Presented to

_____

By

_____

On the Occasion of

_____

Date

_____

TiME OUT

A QUIET-TIME DEVOTIONAL FOR BUSY MOMS

LEIGH ANN THOMAS

BARBOUR
PUBLISHING, INC.
Uhrichsville, Ohio

ISBN 1-57748-720-6

Published by Barbour Publishing, Inc., P.O. Box 719,
Uhrichsville, OH 44683 http://www.barbourbooks.com

 Member of the
Evangelical Christian
Publishers Association

Printed in the United States of America.

DEDICATION

To my husband and best friend, Roy,
and our three awesome gifts,
Laura, Mary, and Katie

How I praise God for you!

ACKNOWLEDGMENTS

- To Barbour Publishing—Thank you for giving me this unique opportunity to share my heart.

- To my sister, Charlene—Knowing you are a phone call away has given me such strength. On those days when chaos seems to reign, thank you for standing in the gap for me. Thank you for pushing me and for insisting that I keep writing. I love you.

- To my mother, Atha Nall—I didn't realize the depth of my love for you until I cradled my own children. Thank you for praying for me. Thank you for teaching me about Jesus. And thank you for being my friend.

INTRODUCTION

Whether working in or outside the home, we all have them—Sidetracked days, Who Me? days, Froot Loops in the Toilet days! We constantly face the question, "Am I doing this right?"

And what is so amazing is that we think we're struggling alone. We assume our peers "have it all together" and that we're the only ones with insecurities. My goal in writing *Time Out— A Quiet-Time Devotional for Busy Moms* is for other mothers to see themselves in its pages and to acknowledge that God's word is our ultimate source of hope and strength. Because in spite of it all, we wouldn't trade the title of "mother" for anything.

So take a few minutes and walk with me through the wonderful, zany, crazy, upside-down world of momhood. And may we be ever mindful that we are never alone; we have a Heavenly Father who loves, guides, supports, and sustains. To Him be the glory!

LEIGH ANN THOMAS

A FORM OF TORTURE

*He gives strength to the weary
and increases the power of the weak.*

ISAIAH 40:29

I've noticed that in old westerns, when the bad guys want to torture their victims, they tie the poor souls up and leave them out in the hot desert sun to die. Every time I see one of these scenes played out, I think of all the unnecessary trouble those outlaws are taking: It would be so much easier to give the unsuspecting victim a two-year-old and shut them up in a room, say about eight feet square, and leave them there for approximately two hours. That would be much more effective torture than merely tying them down in the desert.

My mind actually follows this train of thought each time I spend the morning in a doctor's office with my preschooler. Without fail, by the time I carry my glassy-eyed, feverish angel through the waiting room door, something miraculous happens. Her weak little body suddenly bursts with energy, the fever disappears, and when the doctor comes in, he's not sure who the patient is. The haggard-looking mother seems more likely than the bright-eyed child turning 'round and 'round on his office stool.

I'm learning, though. The next time we make a visit to the doctor, I'll carry paper, crayons, crackers, picture books. . .and a couple of aspirin for myself!

Lord,
this motherhood stuff can be so trying.
Sometimes it seems as if the trials
and aggravations outweigh the joys.
Please give me the strength
and stamina to weather the
not-so-pleasant aspects of being a mom.

And we pray this in order that you may live a life worthy of the Lord and may please him in every way: bearing fruit in every good work, growing in the knowledge of God, being strengthened with all power according to his glorious might so that you may have great endurance and patience, and joyfully giving thanks to the Father, who has qualified you to share in the inheritance of the saints in the kingdom of light.

COLOSSIANS 1:10–12

I WANNA ROCK YOU

But God demonstrates
his own love for us. . . .

ROMANS 5:8

At 5:45 A.M. my eyes pop open, and I am suddenly aware of another presence in our bedroom. Instinct tells me that Mary, our baby, is up early, wanting to be rocked. My husband, Roy, is sleeping soundly, but I have the crazy notion that just maybe, if I pretend I'm asleep, she'll wake him up.

No such luck. I grudgingly crawl out of bed to the whine of "Mommy, I wanna rock you!" With an attitude you could see in the dark, I pick her up and stumble to the living room, where I fall into the rocking chair.

Mary nestles into my arms, her little head on my shoulder. Ever so gently we begin rocking. As she falls back asleep, I can feel her warm baby breath on my neck, and like so many times before, my attitude slowly melts away. The warmth of her little body and the quiet of the house speak to my heart, and there in the darkness I sing silent praise to the God who has given me such a precious gift.

When we hold our children close in our arms, our Heavenly Father's love for us is revealed. He's holding us as we hold them.

Oh Lord,
may I never forget the feel
of Your little ones in my arms.
I praise You for the privilege of
being the instrument of
Your love and care for them.

And I pray that you, being rooted and established in love, may have power, together with all the saints, to grasp how wide and long and high and deep is the love of Christ, and to know this love that surpasses knowledge—that you may be filled to the measure of all the fullness of God.　　　　　　　　　　EPHESIANS 3:17–19

A DAILY DOSE

*I have hidden your word in
my heart that I might not
sin against you.*

PSALM 119:11

I wish someone would invent a "fruit-of-the-Spirit" pill. That way, each morning I could just pop one in, and all day long I would bubble over with love, joy, faith, patience, and so on. I know it would sell. In fact, probably millions of men and children out there would pay any price to purchase a bottle for their wives and mothers. The bottle label could say, "One a day keeps the grouchies away!" My family would be the first to stock up!

Some days I just seem to wake up with my claws extended. I proceed to snap, criticize, and generally spread gloom and frustration. And of course I'm very adept at blaming my sour mood on something or someone else. The culprit is either hormones, lack of sleep, my husband, my children, the price of tea in

China, or all of the above.

By the end of the day, I'm usually so miserable that tears come easily and I'm forced to withdraw for a few moments of self-examination. And almost without fail I discover that the root of the problem is that I've become unplugged—unplugged from the only power source that can conquer daily life as we know it. Maybe I find that I've neglected my quiet time with the Master. Or my priorities may be out of whack because I've taken on too many outside activities. Whatever the specifics, the bottom line is that I should be taking my "fruit-of-the-Spirit pill"—which means quality time spent in prayer and Bible study, seeking God's will.

I praise You, Lord,
for Your faithfulness and forgiveness.
Remind me to give each day to You
so that I may be an instrument
of Your peace.

But the fruit of the Spirit is love, joy, peace, patience, kindness, goodness, faithfulness, gentleness and self-control. Against such things there is no law. GALATIANS 5:22–23

THE TELEPHONE SYNDROME
(Part 1)

*If only you had paid attention
to my commands,
your peace would have been like a river,
your righteousness like the waves of the sea.*

ISAIAH 48:18

A strange phenomenon happens in our home every time I get on the phone. All rules and codes of good behavior suddenly disappear and the children act as if I've stepped into some kind of twilight zone where I cannot possibly see or hear them. They take this opportunity to pick fights, scream loudly, and generally destroy the home I've worked so hard to keep semiclean.

When I get off the phone, my fangs come out. "How dare you behave that way! Couldn't you see me on the phone?" The little darlings cower in their rooms whispering, "What's the matter with Mama?"

SCREAM!

The same type of thing happens in the sixty seconds it takes to run to the mailbox and back. I leave on my mailbox excursion amid smiling cherubs promising to be good—and I return to find the nightmare on Thomas Street. One child will inevitably be strangling the cat, her sister, or both.

I don't have the vaguest idea what this phenomena is called, but the cat and I want answers.

Father,
show me how to instill in my children
a spirit of obedience.
Help me to model a strong character
so that they see the importance of
Christ-like behavior at all times,
even when they think
no one is watching.

"Does the LORD delight in burnt offerings and sacrifices as much as in obeying the voice of the LORD? To obey is better than sacrifice, and to heed is better than the fat of rams."

1 SAMUEL 15:22

THE TELEPHONE SYNDROME

(Part 2)

*If we confess our sins, he is faithful
and just and will forgive us our sins
and purify us from all unrighteousness.*

1 JOHN 1:9

When I was growing up, my brother, sisters, and I would tease our mother about the change of tone in her voice when she answered the phone. She would be giving us the lowdown about some misdeed when the phone would ring. She would answer "Hello?" with the sweetest singsong voice you'd ever heard. We would stare in amazement, wondering who was so deserving of such charm.

I recently asked my family if I had ever done the same thing, expecting that I would receive a great round of applause for the loving and consistent way I treat my loved ones. I stared aghast as all three of them shifted uncomfortably and didn't offer an immediate answer. My husband finally looked at me apologetically and said, "Well, honey, since you asked. . ." I wish I hadn't.

I must admit that I've been known to experience the split-personality syndrome. I can pull up in the church parking lot growling, "Get your feet off the back of my seat now. . . Didn't I tell you not to hit your sister? . . . Why didn't you wash your face, you look like a throwaway!"—and then step out of the car and smile, "Oh, Mrs. So-and-So, you look so pretty today. Yes, it's a beautiful day to worship the Lord!" My poor babies just watch and sigh, probably wishing they could be Mrs. So-and-So for a few moments.

How easy it is to take our loved ones for granted. And yet they of all people deserve the same tact and courtesies we extend to acquaintances and even strangers.

Father,
forgive me for my
inconsistencies as a parent.
Convict my heart to recognize the
uniqueness and value of
each family member.
Help me to be gentle to tender feelings.

"I, even I, am he who blots out your transgressions, for my own sake, and remembers your sins no more."   ISAIAH 43:25

GLAMOUR GIRLS

Charm is deceptive, and beauty is fleeting;
but a woman who fears the LORD is to be praised.

PROVERBS 31:30

With both of us rapidly approaching our thirtieth birthdays, my friend Debbie and I decided that we needed to do something really radical. Something that a youth worker and a church organist would not normally do. With mischief in our eyes, we pondered the possibilities: Run away for the weekend? Disappear forever? After much serious contemplation, we decided to spend an evening with a high-fashion photographer who promised that he could make anyone look absolutely gorgeous.

With plenty of giggles and self-conscious remarks, we went to our appointment wearing no makeup whatsoever. (We were so embarrassed we almost refused to take our sunglasses off.) Then we spent three glorious hours being primped and made over, from lipstick to outrageous outfits to a new hairdo. We had a ball!

It felt so good to be truly glamorous, even if only for one evening!

When we got home, our husbands hardly recognized us, and it took us two days to get all the makeup totally off and the gunk out of our hair. (But we did look good—we have pictures to prove it!)

We women will do amazing things in the name of "looking good." From mud on my face to mayonnaise in my hair, all pride and common sense seem to disappear at the prospect of improving my looks.

My last few years of high school I insisted on bleaching my hair a near-fluorescent blond (much to my mother's horror). The summer after my senior year, with all my newfound maturity, I immediately saw my childish folly and decided to remedy the situation. Armed with a dark brown hair dye kit, I secluded myself in the bathroom only to emerge an hour later with—ta-da!—blue hair.

Many washings later, I reconciled myself to starting my freshman year of college with blue/brown/blond locks. Which really wasn't so bad, considering it was 1980; I gave the impression of being a free spirit, not afraid of making my own fashion statement.

Father,
please help me to spend
as much time seeking Your heart
as I do seeking to improve
my physical appearance.
Create in me a desire for
a gentle and quiet spirit.

Your beauty should not come from outward adornment, such as braided hair and the wearing of gold jewelry and fine clothes. Instead, it should be that of your inner self, the unfading beauty of a gentle and quiet spirit, which is of great worth in God's sight.

1 PETER 3:3–4

COMPELLED
TO PRAY

Do not be anxious about anything,
but in everything, by prayer and petition,
with thanksgiving,
present your requests to God.
And the peace of God,
which transcends all understanding,
will guard your hearts
and your minds in Christ Jesus.

PHILIPPIANS 4:6–7

I don't go very long without a diet soft drink in my hand. When I feel the need for something to drink, nothing gets in my way until my thirst is quenched.

In the same way, sometimes my soul feels so dry that I long to drink in the soothing, soul-quenching grace of the Holy Spirit. The need becomes so strong that I drop what I'm doing and slip away to a private place—the bedroom, the bathroom, or the back porch.

When I go to my Father, I am never disappointed. He reveals to me my innermost self. He shows me the burdens that I thought I had laid at His feet, but which I later took back upon myself. He reminds me of the needs of others, that perhaps I had promised to pray for but didn't. He listens as I confess what He already knew. He restores my soul.

One of my favorite verses is, "For it is God who works in you to will and to act according to his good purpose" (Phil. 2:13). This scripture is full of such excitement and promise! When I have a longing to pray, it's not because of anything I've done. . .but because my Creator is moving in me. What an awesome thought! It never ceases to amaze me that God actually takes the time to notice insignificant me and to draw me closer to Him. What's even more amazing is that to God I'm not insignificant at all. In fact, even when the whole world may be against me, my Lord thinks I'm pretty special. Wow, what a Savior!

Father,
thank You for the gift
and the privilege of prayer.
Thank You for placing within my heart
a longing to know You.

In the same way, the Spirit helps us in our weakness. We do not know what we ought to pray for, but the Spirit himself intercedes for us with groans that words cannot express.

ROMANS 8:26

The Sound
of Music

He put a new song in my mouth,
a hymn of praise to our God.
Many will see and fear
and put their trust in the LORD.

PSALM 40:3

"When others see a shepherd boy, God may see a king. . . ." The wonderful message of Ray Boltz fills the room as I take just a moment to sit down and relax. Nothing ministers to the soul like good Christian music. My sanity has been restored countless times by letting myself go to the musical talents of Sandi Patti, Carman, or Steve and Annie Chapman.

In the same way, nothing adds to a worship service like someone pouring out her heart in song. My friend Jan has an exquisite voice that I could listen to for hours on end. I have heard her speak of the wonderful high she receives from sharing her faith in music.

I have often dreamed of being able to sing like that, to move hearts and minds, touching people's emotions. Someday it won't be just a dream. One day soon, all brothers and sisters in Christ will stand together at the throne of our Lord. As one, we will lift up our voices in a glorious song of praise. What a wonderful day that will be!

One of my greatest joys is joining with other believers in singing the great hymns of old. And oftentimes as I'm going about my daily tasks I find myself humming a hymn I learned as a child. What a wonderful and inspiring way to praise the Lord! Surely He is pleased to see us keep a song in our hearts and His message on our minds.

Thank You, Father,
for the gift of music.
What a joy it has been to
countless believers through the ages.
I look forward with great anticipation
to that glorious day when I
may join with every tribe
and nation as we lift
our voices in praise to You!

Shout for joy to the LORD, all the earth. Worship the LORD with gladness; come before him with joyful songs. Know that the LORD is God. It is he who made us, and we are his; we are his people, the sheep of his pasture. Enter his gates with thanksgiving and his courts with praise; give thanks to him and praise his name. For the LORD is good and his love endures forever; his faithfulness continues through all generations.

PSALM 100

DIVINE PROTECTION

But you are a shield around me,
O LORD;
you bestow glory on me
and lift up my head.

PSALM 3:3

I watched through the living room window as our oldest daughter, Laura, hopped off the school bus. I'd grown to love this time of day, when she would burst breathlessly in the house full of little-girl news. Today, however, as Laura ran toward the house, I noticed something seemed to be moving right behind her. Terror gripped my heart as I realized that what I was seeing was a huge dog, with teeth bared, racing after her.

Without thinking, I flew out the front door and ran toward my daughter, my heart pounding and my fists clenched. I'm not sure what I planned to do; I just knew that animal was not going to hurt my baby! Thankfully, a sharp scream scared the beast away and we hurried safely into the house.

As we came in, however, we heard a horrible gasping sound coming from the kitchen. While I had been rescuing Laura, Mary had gotten the drawstring for the backdoor blinds around her neck. The doormat had slipped out from under her, making her fall, and there wasn't enough slack in the cord for her to go all the way down. She hung there strangling, horror in her little eyes. Quickly, I made my second major rescue for the day, and Mary came out with only a slight bruise. Trembling, I sat down and breathed a prayer of gratitude.

Later that evening I prayed, "Lord, what if I hadn't been there? Would a sitter have known what to do? I can't always be with them; how am I supposed to provide protection?"

God spoke and His answer pierced my heart. *Give them to Me.*

The only way to give my children constant care is by giving them to their Heavenly Father. He is the one who loans our children to us in the first place, and only He can give them divine protection.

Father,
thank You for Your watchful care
over our children.
May I be ever mindful that
as deep as my love is for them,
Your love is immeasurably greater.

"See that you do not look down on one of these little ones. For I tell you that their angels in heaven always see the face of my Father in heaven." MATTHEW 18:10

SLEEP?

Therefore, I urge you, brothers,
in view of God's mercy,
to offer your bodies as living sacrifices,
holy and pleasing to God—
this is your spiritual act of worship.

ROMANS 12:1

I have this fantasy that someday I will crawl into bed and be able to sleep for three whole days—totally undisturbed. Actually, I would be satisfied to sleep past 6 A.M. Motherhood sure changes things. Pleasant memories of staying up late and sleeping all morning seem like a distant, unreal thing of the past.

Sometimes as I crawl out of bed in the mornings, I look back and gaze longingly at my big fluffy pillow and the warm cozy covers. "Oh well," I sigh, "one of these days when the kids are grown, I'm going to sleep late every Saturday for sure." Sure I will. I'll probably lie wide awake remembering how cute the children were when they used to wake me up in the mornings.

Sometimes I'm actually foolhardy enough

to try and nap. That's when the phone starts ringing, the passing motorists decide to let their stereo simulate an outdoor concert, and my conscience kicks in because of all the things that need to be done.

Like I said, I have this fantasy. . . .

Lord,
sometimes it's easy to resent
the demands of motherhood.
My time never seems to be my own.
But, Father,
create in me a spirit of servanthood.
Remind me that as I love
and minister to these little ones,
I'm also serving You.

It is the LORD your God you must follow, and him you must revere. Keep his commands and obey him; serve him and hold fast to him.

DEUTERONOMY 13:4

SECURITY SYSTEM

But the Lord is faithful,
and he will strengthen and
protect you from the evil one.

2 THESSALONIANS 3:3

Some friends of ours recently built a new home and installed a state-of-the-art security system. I have my own unique system I use when my husband, Roy, has to work late at night. He may not get in until the wee hours of the morning, and I've never liked being alone at night. The house suddenly decides to make all kinds of strange groaning noises—noises that never happen when Roy is there.

After the kids are sleeping soundly and I'm ready to turn in, I check all the doors for the fifth time. Then I drag something heavy in front of each one "just in case." I leave on extra lights and then crawl into bed, thanking the Lord that I can trust Him.

Several hours later as I'm sleeping soundly, Roy comes home. He opens the door, slides my barricades out of the way, flips on the TV for a few minutes, grabs a snack, takes a shower, and crawls into bed—without me ever even rolling over! So much for my security system.

I always placed and removed my barricades when the girls were asleep, so I never dreamed that my insecurities were affecting them. One evening, however, after Roy left on a late-night call, I entered the living room to find Laura dragging everything but the kitchen sink in front of the front door.

"What in the world are you doing?" I asked her.

Puzzled, Laura responded, "We don't want anybody to get us, do we, Mama?"

Immediately, I pulled Laura into my arms and apologized for frightening her. Then we prayed together for God's protection and courage. We put our family in His care, and we haven't used any other barricade ever since. (God sure has a way of using our children to wake us up!)

Lord,
my feeble attempts at taking care of
myself must amuse You sometimes.
Please forgive me for
not leaning totally on You.
Help me to point my children
to You as the source of
all hope and strength.
Take away my fears
and fill me with
Your calm assurance.

"For the eyes of the Lord are on the righteous and his ears are attentive to their prayer, but the face of the Lord is against those who do evil."

1 PETER 3:12

Home Business

"Homeworkers Needed! Make big $$$ working from your own home, setting your own hours!" Excited, I tore the ad from the magazine and sent off for more information. At last! A way to make money without leaving home! Wonderful!

An information packet arrived within a week and after perusing the possibilities, I decided to try making beaded earrings for a jewelry company. Oh joy! This was going to be great! According to the brochure, all I had to do was make fifty units (each unit equals one pair) of earrings and I could bring in two hundred dollars to three hundred dollars a week. Wow, why doesn't everyone do this?

With dollar signs dancing in my head, I waited with great anticipation for my first kit of supplies to arrive. I daydreamed about all the nice things I could get for the family with the avalanche of money that was surely on its way. I had serious visions of exotic vacations and a new Jeep Cherokee in the driveway by Christmas.

The day the kit arrived, I grabbed it out of the mailbox and flew into the house. Why waste time?

I cannot express my emotions during that first minute after I dumped the contents of the kit out on the kitchen table. Hundreds upon hundreds of microscopic beads came pouring out. As I wiped beads of perspiration from my forehead, I tried to calm down and think logically. Okay, Leigh Ann, you can do this. You're a semi-intelligent human being.

Two frustrating hours later, my visions of a financial avalanche evaporated as I tearfully admitted defeat. When I looked at the clock, I realized that Roy could walk in at any minute. In a panic, I raked all ten zillion beads back in their package and stashed everything under the bed.

Oh well, Mary's a little too young to whisk off to Europe anyway.

Father,
it's so obvious when I
neglect to seek Your guidance.
Please forgive me for not turning to You
with every decision, great or small.
I pray that my greatest desire
will be to seek Your heart
in all things.

Trust in the LORD with all your heart and lean
not on your own understanding; in all your
ways acknowledge him, and he will make your
paths straight.   PROVERBS 3:5–6

OLD BLUE PICKUP

Give thanks to the LORD,
for he is good;
his love endures forever.

PSALM 107:1

At 5:00 P.M. I'm just getting supper started.
Mary's curled up on the couch watching *Sesame
Street* and Laura's outside riding her bike. I am
filled with the greatest sense of contentment,
anticipating the family coming back together at
the end of the day. My heart is waiting for one
particular sound and the closer it gets to 5:30
P.M. the harder I listen. At last I hear a familiar
hum and the squeak of worn-out brakes as our
old blue pickup pulls up at the mailbox.

The faithful old truck with close to 150,000
miles represents so much more than mere
transportation. To me it is a constant reminder
of the love and sacrifice that flows from my
husband to his family. Roy is the king of
"making do" and he is continually putting off
getting things for himself so that he can do

more for us. He's been known to take on extra work to pay a bill and to wear the same suit in consecutive family pictures—and to do so without complaint. So whenever I get the "discontents" over the furniture or my wardrobe, I think of that old truck, and then I re-evaluate what I really need.

There'll be time for new things later. Right now I need to cherish these days when my husband comes in the door with a wink for me, his arms outstretched to receive two squealing little girls.

Daddy's home!

Father,
please keep my eyes open to
the little joys all around me.
Don't let me miss
the sacredness of everyday life.
Teach me to always keep
a song of thanksgiving
in my heart.

I will sing to the LORD all my life; I will sing praise to my God as long as I live. May my meditation be pleasing to him, as I rejoice in the LORD. PSALM 104:33–34

FROOT LOOPS IN THE TOILET

I can do everything through him who gives me strength.

PHILIPPIANS 4:13

Those who think they must enlist in the navy to have an adventure obviously haven't tried living with preschoolers. Of this I am sure. Some days I wish I could run away and join the armed forces. . . . I'd probably have a better chance of survival.

The day began innocently enough. I pulled Mary down from standing on the windowsills a couple of times—no big deal. I'm beginning to think she's part feline, the way she balances on that two-inch ledge like that. Amazing. Anyway, the girls were playing rather nicely together in Mary's room with only an occasional "Stop it! I'm gonna tell Mama!"

Then, out of nowhere, I heard an awful death cry, a piercing scream, and then another cry that sent chills up my back. As I raced in slow motion the three miles down the hall, I just knew I would round the corner and face blood and broken bones everywhere. (I never for an instant doubted that either girl could pull off a broken bone in her own room.) As I entered the room, an alarming but somewhat comical sight greeted me.

Mary had crawled on top of her little play kitchenette and decided to do a little walking around. When she stepped from the refrigerator to the stove, however, she forgot about the little sink, and down she went—waist deep in a toy kitchen.

To say she was hysterical would be an understatement. I worked frantically for twenty minutes trying to push and/or pull her out, all to no avail. I finally called the church where Roy was at a meeting and left word for him to come home and free his daughter from the kitchen sink. In the meantime, Laura and I kept the captive occupied by opening and closing the little doors at Mary's feet and screaming "peek-a-boo!"

Later that evening, I found Froot Loops in the toilet. But I was too tired to care.

Lord,
on these crazy days when
chaos seems to reign,
help me to keep my sense of humor.
Remind me that these times
are temporary and fleeting.
Help me to keep my eyes on You.

Let us fix our eyes on Jesus, the author and perfecter of our faith, who for the joy set before him endured the cross, scorning its shame, and sat down at the right hand of the throne of God.   HEBREWS 12:2

Making Changes

*Jesus Christ is the same
yesterday and today and forever.*

Hebrews 13:8

I love to make changes. I've always believed that change is good—if it's done with a little forethought. I especially like small, seemingly insignificant changes, like rearranging the furniture. I do this faithfully in at least one room of the house every couple of months. Roy doesn't usually mind as long as I don't touch his computer area. He laid down that law after I slid his desk just a few inches and all those irritating cables and wires and stuff came unplugged. Talk about sensitive. . . .

I usually tackle bigger changes when Roy's out of town, like painting something or putting up a wallpaper strip. He always praises me when he arrives home, then a few days later he subtly hints that maybe pink roses aren't exactly the most masculine things I could have pasted on our bedroom wall. Oh well. . . .

These days our lives are in a constant state of change. Children grow, careers are redefined, friendships are made, goals are established and reestablished. It seems as if the ground is always shifting beneath us. The world pulls and pushes, scoffs and laughs at the Christian family. Society is forever redefining "what's in," ridiculing the tried and true values of the Christ-like life. Our culture screams at us to follow or fall behind and defies us to seek the way of Truth.

In all of the chaos the world hurls our way, isn't it wonderful that our God never changes? The God who loved and fellowshipped with Abraham and Sarah is the same God who loves and desires fellowship with us. What a wonder. What a comfort!

Oh Father,
thank You for the firm foundation
that You offer us through Your Son.
Thank You for the knowledge
that we are forever secure in
Your unfailing love.
Thank You, Father,
that You never change.

For I am convinced that neither death nor life, neither angels nor demons, neither the present nor the future, nor any powers, neither height nor depth, nor anything else in all creation, will be able to separate us from the love of God that is in Christ Jesus our Lord.

ROMANS 8:38–39

PRIVACY?

Not only so,
but we also rejoice in our sufferings,
because we know that
suffering produces perseverance;
perseverance, character;
and character, hope.

ROMANS 5:3–4

There are certain impossibilities associated with motherhood: sleep, quiet, and being able to go to the bathroom by yourself. It seems to me that one of our basic human rights should include being able to stay in the bathroom for four solid minutes—undisturbed. Not so. I gave up that right in the delivery room.

Last night after supper, the family was relaxing, each of them apparently completely occupied. Roy was reading the paper, and the girls were constructing a tower of books on the floor. I quietly excused myself and made my way down the hall to the Thomas powder room. I entered the room, shut the door, and (this is no exaggeration) was interrupted a whopping total of five times in the next four minutes.

A typical exchange through the bathroom door goes something like this:

Husband: "Honey, the phone's ringing, do you want me to get it?"

(I don't bother answering that one.)

Child: "Mommy, Mary's not playing right!"

Other child: "I am so!"

Child: "No she's not!"

Harassed mother: "Girls, I'll be out in a minute; go back and play."

Child: "But. . ."

Harassed mother: "No buts; go on and play!"

(Pause.)

Other child: "Mommy, I'm hungry."

Harassed mother: "You couldn't be hungry, we just had dinner, now go on. . .I told you I'd be out in a few minutes."

(Pause.)

Child: "Mommy, are you coming out soon?"

I finally started locking myself in—but then the girls created a game of sticking their fingers under the door and asking me if I'd try to catch them.

Oh Lord,
sometimes holding my breath and
counting to ten just doesn't do it.
I need patience!
Actually, Lord,
I need a little space—
just a few moments now and then
that I can call my own.
Help me to effectively
communicate this need to
my family so that they can
also benefit from a less
stressed-out mom.

Be joyful always; pray continually; give thanks in all circumstances, for this is God's will for you in Christ Jesus.

1 THESSALONIANS 5:16–18

HIS PRECIOUS HANDS

*Blessed is the man who
fears the LORD,
who finds great delight in
his commands.*

PSALM 112:1

In the early years of our marriage, I seemed to have one major goal—to "repair" my husband. He was never neat enough, attentive enough, spontaneous enough. . . . You get the picture. I was determined (by brute force if necessary) to mold and shape him into the perfect life companion. The only problem was, Roy didn't realize he needed a character makeover.

Can you say "conflict"?

Then one year we attended a marriage enrichment weekend that put my compulsions to change him into a new perspective. We all sat in chairs facing each other, and then one at a time we each took our spouse's hands, looked at them, and thought of all that those hands do for us day by day.

Emotion overwhelmed me as I took Roy's hands in mine. All my ridiculous grievances melted away, and I genuinely and humbly looked at what the Lord had given me, perhaps for the first time. Those wonderful hands had always held me in gentleness and love, never in anger. They had calmed me down when I was upset. They had faithfully worked to earn a living to support a family. They had reached out to neighborhood children to take them to church and bring them to Christ. They had loved, held, played with, and tickled our own children. They had mowed the grass, taken out the trash, painted the house, fixed the car, pushed a stroller, applied first aid, and wiped away tears. And the owner of those hands had always driven his family to church and led them in worship.

I finally realized that God didn't bless me with a husband just so I could "repair" him. He gave me a wonderful gentle man to love and honor in the Lord. He gave me someone with whom to work, laugh and cry, and raise a Christian family.

So now when little irritations threaten to cloud my marital bliss, I do my very best to close my eyes and think of those blessed hands. Try it—it works wonders!

⎯⎯⎯

Father,
thank You so much for
giving me a life partner.
You've given me a sweetheart
and a best friend.
I lift my husband up to You, Lord,
and I pray that he will continue
to grow in Your strength and wisdom.

⎯⎯⎯

Blessed is the man who does not walk in the counsel of the wicked or stand in the way of sinners or sit in the seat of mockers. But his delight is in the law of the LORD, and on his law he meditates day and night.   PSALM 1:1–2

THOSE WHITE-HAIRED SAINTS

*"Blessed are those who mourn,
for they will be comforted."*

MATTHEW 5:4

Most churches have at least one or two of them: those wonderful women with the kind of inner beauty that comes only from above. They have been tested by fire and have emerged strong, faithful, and true to their relationship with God. They have a presence that draws you in, a certain gentle holiness about them. They are exceedingly rare and precious, and they are truly a gift from God to the rest of us.

Erelene Sykes is one of these godly women with whom my own church is blessed. When I joined the church a few years ago, before long I saw that Mrs. Erelene exuded the kind of strength and wisdom that comes from a continuous spiritual pilgrimage. But I recently discovered even more of her treasures.

When we announced that a third child was on the way, both our own family and our church family were very excited. Laura and Mary were especially filled with anticipation.

So you can imagine my heartache when after two healthy pregnancies, I began experiencing problems with this one. Finally, in my third month of pregnancy, I suffered a miscarriage.

I was stunned. How could this have happened? I had actually seen the little heartbeat only a week before, and I had immediately fallen in love with this new little life. The doctor had given me a "baby's first picture" from the ultrasound, which I had proudly displayed to friends and strangers alike. Why had this happened? My head was spinning with unanswered questions.

God sent His strength and comfort through Roy, my family, friends—and through Mrs. Erelene. She gave me time to grieve, and then she shared with me how thirty years earlier she had experienced the same pain three times over. As she shared her own healing process, she helped me realize that I wouldn't want to call our baby back to his or her earthly body of clay. Our little one was now experiencing the joys of heaven instead of the sorrows of this world.

Mrs. Erelene let herself be an instrument of comfort, and for that I am eternally grateful. Immersed in the daily bumblings of my life, I can't imagine myself becoming a saintly woman of wisdom. But becoming a saint doesn't depend on my imagination; it depends on Christ's grace. My goal, with God's grace, is to go steadily on in my spiritual pilgrimage, so that I, too, may "comfort others with the comfort I have received." And on that blessed day when I see my Savior face to face, I pray I will hear: "Well done, thou good and faithful servant."

Father,
some things are so hard to understand.
There are times when tears cloud
my vision and I can't see Your hand in
my life. But through these times, Lord,
I know You love me—
and I place my faith
and trust in that love.
And, Father, I thank You for the tender
comfort of one of Your saints.
As she continues her walk with You,
I ask for Your blessing on her life.

Praise be to the God and Father of our Lord
Jesus Christ, the Father of compassion and the
God of all comfort, who comforts us in all our
troubles, so that we can comfort those in any
trouble with the comfort we ourselves have
received from God.   2 CORINTHIANS 1:3–4

BETWEEN LAUGHTER AND TEARS

*Therefore,
since we have been justified
through faith, we have
peace with God through
our Lord Jesus Christ.*

ROMANS 5:1

It was raining and the girls were restless—not a good combination. They insisted that they had nothing with which to amuse themselves in their room full of toys, and I was determined that they would not spend a mindless afternoon in front of the television. After the hundredth "What can we do now?" I decided that something major had to be done, so I pulled out the big guns. "Okay, kids, let's go shopping!" (The Thomas family's answer to restlessness.)

Determined to have a successful outing, I made sure that everyone was fed and had last-minute bathroom opportunities. After ten solid minutes of scrambling for shoes and coats, we finally started off on our big adventure. Big mistake. Each gallon-sized drop of rain that pelted us seemed to scream, "Stay home! Stay home!" How I wish I had listened.

As we burst into our local department store, I suddenly realized I was completely void of cash. With teeth clenched, we braved the elements once again long enough to whiz over to the bank. (I use the word "whiz" loosely.) To make a long painful story short and painful, while one child complained about being wet and uncomfortable, the other child decided to throw up all over the back seat. To wrap up our delightful little excursion, the instant cash machine wasn't working and the drive-through was closed.

I couldn't decide whether to laugh or cry, so we returned home, cleaned up, and drowned our frustrations in—yes—popcorn and a video.

Father,
I'm learning that being a
mom is never simple.
Things rarely work out as planned.
But thank You, Father,
for being my source of strength
and for calming my soul when
frustrations seem to reign.

"Peace I leave with you; my peace I give you. I do not give to you as the world gives. Do not let your hearts be troubled and do not be afraid."

JOHN 14:27

No Greater Joy

*"Let the little children come to me,
and do not hinder them,
for the kingdom of God
belongs to such as these."*

MARK 10:14

Even in the months before our children made their grand entrance into the world, Roy and I prayed for them. Our prayers centered on the hope that at the right time in their lives they would make a personal decision for Christ. As Laura grew older, our prayers became even more fervent. In fact, we were so busy praying, that we came dangerously close to not recognizing the answer.

At the age of six, Laura would ask an occasional question such as, "How old do I have to be before I can be a Christian?" We would smile and say, "You'll know, honey. Jesus will let you know." At the age of seven, she became more persistent and finally stated point blank, "I want to be a Christian." Roy and I were concerned about Laura being so young, but we sat down with her and read from the Bible about God's plan of salvation. We explained to Laura what an important decision this was, and we asked her to say in her own words what she thought accepting Christ meant. We then asked Laura to take a few days to search her heart and to make sure she was ready. A couple of days later Laura quietly approached me and said, "Mama, I want to ask Jesus in my heart."

Patiently I responded, "Well, honey, we wanted you to pray about it."

"Mama, I did."

"Well, honey, what did you say to Jesus?"

"I told Him that I wanted to be a Christian, but that I was waiting for you and Daddy to let me."

Ouch! I felt so foolish. We had been busy making sure the time was right in our minds, and meanwhile we were ignoring the fact that the Spirit was working in Laura's heart.

I called to Roy to come inside, and the three of us knelt by the bed in Laura's room. With tears streaming and hearts pounding, a father, mother, and child came into the presence of their Creator, while a small, fragile voice prayed the sinner's prayer. Never in my life had I felt so close to the doors of heaven. And I knew in my heart that there was truly "no greater joy."

O precious Lord,
thank You for the salvation of our baby!
Please give us wisdom
as Christian parents.
Show us how to guide and nurture
this child in Your ways,
that she may remain
strong and true to You.

I have no greater joy than to hear that my children are walking in the truth.   3 JOHN 4

GROWING UP,
LETTING GO

And it will be said:
"Build up, build up,
prepare the road!
Remove the obstacles
out of the way of my people."

ISAIAH 57:14

"I can do it by myself!"

"I know you can, honey, but Mommy just wants to help you."

"I don't need your help!"

I've dreamed of this moment for years—the time when the girls would actually start doing more for themselves—a time when I wouldn't feel like I was waiting on them hand and foot. But now that this longed-for occasion has arrived, something just does not feel quite right. I feel as if I'm losing something, like something precious is slipping away.

In fact, the longer that I'm a mother, the

more I see that this vague feeling of loss is a continuous process. From their infancy until the present, our children's level of dependency on Roy and me has changed dramatically. They used to be content to cuddle up on our laps for a story; now they'd rather have friends over to play. They used to run and jump in their daddy's arms when he walked in the door from work; now the oldest sometimes doesn't look up from what she's doing.

As parents, we knew this would happen. In fact, we prayed that our children would grow up to be strong, independent adults. But it still isn't easy to let go.

I'll never forget Laura's first day of school. My legs were like lead as I walked away and left her in a classroom of near strangers. My vision was cloudy with tears and I knew I had to get out of there fast before everyone saw Laura's mommy cry like a baby. My heart was heavy for several days—but it did get easier.

Of course when Mary starts "big school," I'll experience it all over again, but that's all right. All these little "letting go's" are preparing me for the big ones later on. And I know that when the day arrives and the girls walk away into college, marriage, or a career, I'll feel pretty much the same way. And I'll breathe pretty much the same prayer, "Oh God, how I love these girls. . .please take care of them for us!"

Oh Father,
the girls are growing up so quickly.
I'm beginning to see just how
short-lived our time is together.
Guide me as I strive
to make our home a haven—
a place of love, joy,
and rest from this world—
so that no matter how far they go,
they can always depend on
the love-light of home.

Train a child in the way he should go, and when he is old he will not turn from it.

PROVERBS 22:6

LOADED QUESTIONS

Teach me to do your will,
for you are my God;
may your good Spirit lead me
on level ground.

PSALM 143:10

I've done it again. I've put that hunted, trapped look on Roy's face. Good grief, I just wanted an honest answer to a simple question. I didn't realize that I was asking so much. But his pained expression tells me my latest loaded question has set a new record.

All I said was, "Honey, if I died, how soon do you think you'd remarry?" and he acted as if I had said, "Honey, I'm going to destroy the computer or the television set; which would you prefer?"

He finally responded. "I wouldn't remarry, honey. No one could ever take your place."

"Yes, you would. Anyway, I want the girls to have a mother."

"Honey, I can't even imagine being married to someone else."

(Satisfied smile.) "Thanks, honey. . .me, too. (Pause.) So. . .how long would you wait?"

I know I've gone too far when he sighs deeply and mutters something about needing to change the oil in the car.

I have a history of creating these sorts of conversations. Other hall-of-famers include: "Do you think this dress makes me look fat?" "Do you think I'm starting to look old?" "Is there anything you would change about me?"

Roy probably thinks I derive some sort of deranged pleasure from watching him squirm. He might suspect that I don't even want an honest answer. . . . I think I'll ask him.

Oh Father,
how many times have I
come to You under the pretense
of seeking Your guidance—
and then gone my own way?
Give me a yearning for
the honesty and purity of heart
that only Your light can give.
Don't let me cater to vanity
and shallow living when there is
so much reality to be lived in You.

If any of you lacks wisdom, he should ask God, who gives generously to all without finding fault, and it will be given to him.

JAMES 1:5

Who Me?

Being confident of this,
that he who began a good work
in you will carry it on
to completion until
the day of Christ Jesus.

PHILIPPIANS 1:6

The hardest thing for me to accept in my Christian walk is that Almighty God, Creator of heaven and earth, actually has a plan and a life's work prepared for me. It's so much easier to believe and rejoice in how He's working in other lives. You know, other more "qualified" people. I have no problem believing in the life, death, and resurrection of Jesus Christ. I believe He loved this world enough to pay the ultimate price for our sin by laying down His life. But for some reason, I sometimes have trouble believing that He wants to use *me*. I feel inadequate so much of the time. I mean, I've been known to snap at my children and be angry with my husband. My house is a mess, I bite my nails, and sometimes I speak before I think. How can God use me when I feel so incompetent?

When feelings of inadequacy threaten to overwhelm me, I cling to the Scriptures. I read about those men and women in Bible times who God used to carry out His will. I think about Moses, who used his speech defect as an excuse to God. I think of David, who was only a shepherd boy. And then there was Sarah, who laughed when God's messengers said she was to bear a child, and Rebekah, who encouraged her own son to be deceitful to his father. In spite of their human frailties, God used these men and women and many others to accomplish His purposes.

So let us remind ourselves often: God can use me; God can use you. All He requires is a willing heart, totally committed to Him.

Lord,
I am in constant awe of
Your patience and grace.
Thank You for using me in
my weakness to further Your kingdom.
I praise You, Lord,
for Your strength and Your love.

But he said to me, "My grace is sufficient for you, for my power is made perfect in weakness." Therefore I will boast all the more gladly about my weaknesses, so that Christ's power may rest on me.   2 CORINTHIANS 12:9

THE GREAT OUTDOORS

"How often I have longed to gather your children together, as a hen gathers her chicks under her wings."

MATTHEW 23:37

I have wonderful childhood memories of family camping trips. The much-anticipated vacations were always an adventure. Our big blue canvas tent was the site of many late-night storytelling sessions, tickle-fights, and flashlight games. As I grew up and our family expanded, Mom and Dad abandoned the tent for a camper that sat on the back of Dad's pickup. A few years later we advanced to the ultimate—a deluxe pop-up version that we pulled behind the truck. What we camped in, however, was irrelevant. The important thing was that we kids had Mom and Dad's undivided attention, in a small space, for extended periods of time. It was great. All rules and codes of conduct relaxed a little, while we concentrated on enjoying each other as a family.

I carried these precious memories with me into marriage, so when Roy and I thought the girls were old enough, we decided the time had come for them to experience the great outdoors for themselves. Something, however, went terribly wrong. Camping as an adult just wasn't the same exhilarating experience that it had been when I was a child. For one thing, midnight trips to the bathhouse were a major bummer. And where did all those mosquitoes come from? I also made another major discovery: The ground is harder now than it was twenty years ago. And family togetherness is wonderful, but not when you're trapped together for twenty-four hours in a space approximately eight feet by ten feet during a thunderstorm. I guess that's what we deserve for cramming a four-member family into a three-man tent.

Oh well, our experiences haven't been that bad. In fact, when we look at pictures taken during our trips, we look like we're having the time of our lives. The pictures capture the memory of fun and laughter, not sand, bugs, and rainy nights.

Maybe next year we could try camping in the mountains. It shouldn't be as hot and sandy, and this time we'll be sure to pack an air mattress for Mom.

Lord,
don't let us forget
just how important it is to
spend time together as a family.
And as we create these
precious memories with the children,
may every experience
guide them closer to You.

Unless the LORD builds the house, its builders labor in vain. PSALM 127:1

TRAIN OF THOUGHT

I wait for the LORD,
my soul waits,
and in his word I put my hope.

PSALM 130:5

I want another baby.

No, I don't.

Yes, I really do. They're so precious and they feel so good.

But they cry a lot and they're so much work. I'd be crazy to have another baby. It would be like starting all over. Mary will be in school soon, and I can go back to work and bring in more money.

But they're so soft and sweet. And I just love baby feet. I always have. Fingers and ears are adorable, but there's just something about baby feet.

I must be insane. What about sleepless nights, bottles, and diapers? And I'm not twenty-three anymore; I haven't been for some time. I don't want to be mistaken for my child's grandmother. And what will everyone think? In today's world if you have more than two children, people wonder what your problem is. "Haven't you heard of birth control?"

I don't care what people think.

But what if. . .I miscarry again? Now that I know something can go wrong. . .

With all my heart I want another child. Period.

Oh Father,
with my entire being
I ask You for another child.
But I'm so scared, Lord.
Please show me how to
leave my fears at Your feet.
Help me to trust You
and to know that You alone know
what is best for this family.
I turn it all over to You, Lord.
Your will be done.

You will keep in perfect peace him whose mind is steadfast, because he trusts in you.

ISAIAH 26:3

MOTHER'S DAY

*Sons are a heritage
from the LORD,
children a reward
from him.*

PSALM 127:3

I love Mother's Day, if only because the girls' secretive excitement is so much fun to watch. Okay, so I like the gifts, too. I can't help it; I'm only human and presents are fun. Especially Mother's Day presents: finger paintings, handprints, homemade jewelry, confections of every sort, pencil holders, place mats. Each masterpiece is crafted with such love that its value is immeasurable.

The days leading up to Mom's big event are also exciting. I can't walk down the hall without hearing, "Mama, don't look!" and then a quick slam of a bedroom door. The last-minute shopping trip with Daddy is also a yearly tradition. One or two days in advance, my family all proudly announces that they need to run uptown to "run some errands." Grinning from ear to ear, they hop in Dad's truck, waving and blowing kisses, assuming that Mom couldn't possibly know what they are up to. An hour or two later they burst into the house with shouts of "Mama, close your eyes!" Then they seclude themselves in their rooms among sounds of wrapping paper and tape being pulled off the roll. They emerge sometime later with those same precious grins, their eyes wide with innocence. "Mama, you can't go in our room, okay?"

"Okay," I promise. *I hope they have things hidden well. I'd hate to stumble onto something when I check on them tonight.*

Lord,
thank You for my family.
Thank You for special days.
Thank You for the sound of
little voices and for
childish expressions of love.

Give thanks to the Lord, for he is good; his
love endures forever. PSALM 107:1

ETERNAL INSTANTS

*Your faithfulness continues
through all generations;
you established the earth,
and it endures.*

PSALM 119:90

In his book *God Came Near* (Multnomah Press, 1987), Max Lucado talks about eternal instants. Those precious times when God reveals the value of the moment. When a seemingly ordinary event takes on eternal significance. Those fleeting seconds when your little one turns and whispers, "I love you, Mama," and you catch your breath and whisper back on a wave of emotion, "I love you, too, baby."

I'm learning that God uses these instants to reveal Himself and His purposes. As He speaks, He brings comfort and strength, and He prepares our hearts for things to come.

The morning after the miscarriage of our little one, as we began to grieve, Roy led me through a local park. God used the beauty of

His creation to reach my hurting soul. The sunlight sparkled brilliantly through my tears, and the warm, soothing breeze encircled my exhausted body. God spoke to our breaking hearts. We listened. We prayed. We began the long process of healing.

In yet another eternal instant, after learning that a dear friend was moving away, God spoke through a hymn we were singing in church. I had already sung several verses before I realized that the Master was trying to get my attention. The inspiring words of "Great Is Thy Faithfulness" seeped into my consciousness, and I joyfully laid my burden at the Lord's feet.

Oh how God will speak to the listening heart!

Great is Thy faithfulness,
* O God my Father,*
There is no shadow of turning with Thee;
* Thou changest not,*
Thy compassions, they fail not;
* As Thou hast been Thou forever*
* wilt be.*
Great is Thy faithfulness!
* Great is Thy faithfulness!*
Morning by morning new mercies I see;
* All I have needed Thy hand hath*
* provided;*
Great is Thy faithfulness,
* Lord, unto me!*

THOMAS O. CHISHOLM

Know therefore that the Lord your God is God; he is the faithful God, keeping his covenant of love to a thousand generations of those who love him and keep his commands.

DEUTERONOMY 7:9

THE GIFT OF LIFE

From birth I have relied on you;
you brought me forth from
my mother's womb.
I will ever praise you.

PSALM 71:6

You would think that this was my first pregnancy, not my fourth; I am filled with such a sense of excitement and anticipation. Everything feels so new. Every kick and prod, every roll and tumble that this child delivers, fills me with awe. I am consumed with the yearning to hold and cuddle, to nurture, to bring this little person into a family eagerly awaiting the opportunity to love someone new.

Even with three more months of waiting, I am almost obsessed with thoughts of being ready. I am absurdly giddy over recent purchases—bottles, burp cloths, diapers. Friends watch and smile and shake their heads. "She's done all this before, what's the big deal?"

I'm not quite sure. Maybe I'm cherishing

this experience so much because I know the pain of losing a life. Maybe it's the realization that I'm not getting any younger, and this may be our last child. Or maybe it's because I'm walking closer to my Lord than ever before, and I'm seeing the miracle of life through new eyes.

Whatever the reason, through it all—the discomfort, the nausea, the sickness, the aches and pains—I am always aware of the miracle growing within me. When I close my eyes, I can hear the fragile heartbeat and feel the tiny fingers in mine. And I praise my Creator for the gift of motherhood—and for the privilege and honor of serving Him in this way.

Oh Father,
with my whole heart I thank You
and I praise You for the life within me.
I lift this child up to You, Lord,
and I pray that he or she
will seek Your heart.

For you created my inmost being; you knit me together in my mother's womb. I praise you because I am fearfully and wonderfully made; your works are wonderful, I know that full well.

PSALM 139:13–14

Too Cool

Listen, my son,
and be wise,
and keep your heart
on the right path.

PROVERBS 23:19

As a teenager I was constantly exasperated by my totally uncool parents. They just didn't understand what life was really all about. So at the wise old age of seventeen, I vowed that if and when I had children, I would be the perfect example of a cool parent. I would be patient, kind, loving, and extremely understanding. I would be the ultimate listener, friend, and confidante. I would be a shining beacon of motherhood to all the world.

My plan worked flawlessly. . .until my children were actually born. Keeping my cool suddenly became far more important than being cool. I mean, who has time to keep up with "what's happening" when you're swallowed up by laundry, potty training, and maintaining some degree of sanity? Certainly not me.

So maybe my mom wasn't so bad. . . . After all, there was the time a boy was thirty minutes late to pick me up for a date, and Mom, seeing I was on the verge of hysteria, had this wonderful idea. She piled me and my brother and sisters in the car and rode around for another half hour, so that if my date should show up looking for me, it would look like I had stood him up! It took a very wise mother to restore her daughter's hurt pride that day.

Now that's cool!

Lord,
I praise You and I thank you
for the privilege of being raised
in a Christian home.
May our hearts keep You
the center of our lives so that
our girls may also experience
the joy and acceptance of living
in a Christ-centered home.

Love the Lord your God with all your heart and
with all your soul and with all your strength.
These commandments that I give you today are
to be upon your hearts. Impress them on your
children. Talk about them when you sit at home
and when you walk along the road, when you lie
down and when you get up. Tie them as symbols
on your hands and bind them on your foreheads.
Write them on the doorframes of your houses
and on your gates.   DEUTERONOMY 6:5–9

Legacy
of Faith

*Only be careful and
watch yourselves closely
so that you do not forget
the things your eyes have seen
or let them slip from
your heart as long as you live.
Teach them to your children
and to their children after them.*
Deuteronomy 4:9

Granny. What a dear precious word. And what a dear is this woman before me now. Still and pale, her breathing is labored. A small tube brings her relief from the pain.

Fifty-five years ago she was also in pain. But that pain gave birth to joy as she lovingly cradled her newborn son. Fifty-five years ago, she was a young mother with hopes and dreams, plans and visions, who gave every waking thought to her husband and children.

Today's pain is vastly different. Cancer destroys the once strong and vibrant body. But even cancer's merciless destruction cannot touch Granny's beauty. For now, just as it was fifty-five years ago, her every waking thought is of those she loves. Even now she yearns for her life's love, who also suffers from the same dreaded disease.

Her legacy can be seen in the sea of concerned faces around her: a whispered prayer, the light of a smile, a joke told to lift spirits; all of these are qualities given to her by her Lord, and she has unselfishly passed them on to her family.

As I hold her precious, fragile hand, I am overcome with gratitude, for I realize that I am a small part of a beautiful legacy of faith. The unwavering truths that were taught to my dad by Gramps and Granny I now instill in my children. And my constant hope and prayer is that the solid foundation my family enjoys now will be cherished by generations to come.

I thank You, Lord,
for Your master plan—
and for this woman of love
who encouraged in my father
the faith I now share with my children.
Be with my grandparents, Lord.
Comfort them and give them strength.
And let them feel from us
the love and encouragement
they have so willingly given.

Praise be to the God and Father of our Lord Jesus Christ! In his great mercy he has given us new birth into a living hope through the resurrection of Jesus Christ from the dead, and into an inheritance that can never perish, spoil or fade—kept in heaven for you.

1 PETER 1:3–4

No End in Sight

*He gives strength
to the weary.*

Isaiah 40:29

It's official. I'm going to be pregnant forever.
The kind folks from Guinness will be here any
day now, eager to include me in their next
edition of world records.

I've had it. It's hot, and I'm tired and whiney.
I usually enjoy being a southern gal, but after
twenty-eight straight days of 90-plus degree
weather with a heat index of over 100, I'd be
willing to be a Yankee any day.

I can't sleep because I need to go to the
bathroom five times a night. And when I do
finally fall asleep and I attempt to roll over, Roy
bolts upright with, "What's the matter, honey?
Are you okay?" After my assurances that I was
just turning over and not actually giving birth, he
lies back down muttering, "Good grief."

I'm always hungry, but I don't know what I
want. I'm mad and irritable, but I'm not sure at

whom, so I take it out on my poor family. Normal childhood offenses become cause for major motherly overreactions. My precious spouse and children resort to tiptoeing around the house, fearful of my next explosion. In fact, I'm pretty sure I overheard them praying that the baby would come soon and the monster invading Mom's body would go away.

It also doesn't help when people say, "You haven't had that baby yet?" or "Feeling fat and sassy, are we?" or "Hey, fat mama!" I want to respond with something witty, but I need all my willpower not to slug them.

Thankfully, pregnancy is only a temporary condition. Looking back at my first two, I have little or no unpleasant memories. Somehow, holding that new little life will erase all thoughts of discomfort. And hopefully my family will come through with as few battle scars as possible.

Father,
help me not to get
so bogged down in the discomfort
of the moment that
I lose sight of the joy to come.
Strengthen me as
I prepare to welcome
this tiny treasure into the world.

But those who hope in the LORD will renew their strength. They will soar on wings like eagles; they will run and not grow weary, they will walk and not be faint. ISAIAH 40:31

LABOR DAY

*"I prayed for this child, and the LORD
has granted me what I asked of him."*

1 SAMUEL 1:27

When you're pregnant, you learn that there are as
many different childbirth stories as there are
children in the world. And like so many things
God designed, no two stories are exactly alike.
Accounts vary from the dramatic to the amazing,
from the incredibly short, barely-made-it-to-
the-hospital, to hours upon hours of will-this-
child-ever-come?

My first labor (the preamble to Miss Laura
Elizabeth) began with all of the excitement and
anticipation that comes with a first pregnancy.
My beginning hours in the hospital were so
effortless that Roy and I actually laughed and
joked about how easy it was, scoffing at all the
horror stories we had endured. We obviously
knew what we were doing, right? I mean, how
hard could it be? Here I was handling these little
bitty contractions like a pro, while at the same

time I took pictures of my husband dressed up in green doctor's scrubs.

Of course fourteen hours later I was completely out of my head and begging the nurses, "Please just hit me on the head with a hammer."

In comparison, Miss Mary Catherine's arrival was a breeze. Within an hour and a half after checking in at the hospital, I was cradling nine pounds and six ounces of beautiful baby girl. Of course during that brief time I was also slightly dopey with pain medication. I distinctly remember telling the doctor that I loved him.

Miss Katie Leigh's entrance was equally original. Labor was induced and small contractions seemed to drag on endlessly. Not until Roy and my nurse decided to take a lunch break did Miss Katie decide she was coming immediately. While my mom ran for help, our pastor ran to find Roy (who was calmly eating a chicken sandwich in the cafeteria). Everyone made it with about three minutes to spare, and I was soon holding my third precious bundle.

Although different in the details, each experience was equally awesome. We heard each announcement of "It's a girl!" as if for the first time. Clutching our precious newborns, Roy and

I wept and prayed and lifted up voices of thanks-giving and praise to our blessed Creator.

Oh Lord,
as I cradle Your new creation,
I can't seem to stop crying
tears of pure joy.
Mere words seem inadequate
to describe the beautiful ache
in my heart.
I feel so unworthy, Father.
Guide me, love me, be with me,
and grant me wisdom as I strive
to mother this precious child.

"A woman giving birth to a child has pain because her time has come; but when her baby is born she forgets the anguish because of her joy that a child is born into the world."

JOHN 16:21

OLDIES?

Keep my commands in your heart,
for they will prolong your life
many years and
bring you prosperity.

PROVERBS 3:1–2

The day was warm and beautiful so I lowered
the car window on my way through town. I was
enjoying a rare morning alone and I was in
especially good spirits. Hitting the "scan"
button on the radio, I settled back to wait for
something upbeat to match my mood. To my
delight, one of my favorite songs from my
school days broke through the airwaves and
filled the car. Feeling like a schoolgirl again, I
ignored the smirks from neighboring cars as I
sang along with the singer in a little kareoke-
type fun. *I love that song,* I thought. I couldn't
have felt more relaxed and carefree until I
heard, "Thanks for listening to your favorite
oldies. . .have a great day!"

What?! Oldies? They must be mistaken. My

music couldn't be considered oldies, could it?

That experience reminded me of the first time I was ma'am'ed. (You know, yes, ma'am—no, ma'am.) I was cruising through a drive-thru when an underage worker (she had to be) said, "Yes, ma'am," to my request for ketchup. I quickly glanced over my shoulder before I remembered no one else was in the car. *She's probably just being polite,* I reasoned.

I've finally come to the conclusion that the D.J. was having an off day and the teenybopper in the drive-thru wasn't raised right. (I mean, she really should be taught that it's rude to ma'am someone so young. . . don'tcha think?)

Father,
help me to greet each passing year
with grace and dignity.
May I take the focus off of
"losing my youth"
and focus on what is gained:
wisdom, maturity,
a closer walk with You,
and experiences that can be shared.

She speaks with wisdom, and faithful instruction is on her tongue. She watches over the affairs of her household and does not eat the bread of idleness. Her children arise and call her blessed; her husband also, and he praises her.   PROVERBS 31: 26–28

OVERWHELMED

*It is God who
arms me with strength
and makes my way perfect.*

PSALM 18:32

It has happened countless times. I awake with a yawn, a stretch, and a smile. I roll over and hug my pillow, burying my face in its softness. As I relish those last few moments in the covers' warmth, my thoughts turn sleepily to the day ahead. I enjoy several seconds of cheerful anticipation. . .before it happens.

My brain immediately shifts into overdrive as the weight and burdens of the day's responsibilities settle on me. Resentment seeps in as I think of all the activities competing for my time. Housework beckons. Children demand. Deadlines loom. Promises must be kept. Appointments must be met. Potential joy is shattered as I yield to selfishness. I greet the new day with a grumble in my heart and a discontented frown on my face.

The day then proceeds pretty much as expected. The housework seems endless and the children are unusually demanding. The entire morning seems to be spent taking one step forward and two giant leaps backward. Stubbornly I question, *What in the world went wrong?*

And every time I face the question honestly, I immediately realize that I took the wrong path hours ago. Right after I savor that first morning stretch, my waking thoughts have a choice to make. And the path I too often take is self's. I choose to go my own way—and I end up stumbling around, tripping over worldly thoughts and attitudes. My sense of perspective disappears as I look at life through my eyes.

What's missing is God's ways: His thoughts, His eyes. Without fail, when I neglect to give each day's burdens to Him, I inevitably carry them around myself. And the results can be disastrous, including not only the loss of my joy, but the loss of my fellowship with Him and with others.

Of course housework will still beckon and children will still demand, but when the day is given to the Lord, selfish thoughts can be replaced with the joy of servanthood.

Father,
I thank You for each new day.
May I always be aware that it is
a priceless gift from You.
Remind me to turn
my first waking thoughts
to You and Your ways,
so that I may walk
in Your strength and not my own.

Praise be to the Lord, to God our Savior, who
daily bears our burdens.　　　　PSALM 68:19

FRIENDS

A friend loves at all times,
and a brother is born
for adversity.

PROVERBS 17:17

It had been a long day and I had had enough. Katie had dumped three consecutive cups of cereal on the floor. She ran from me every time her diaper needed changing, yet she cried from being uncomfortable. Laura "misplaced" Mary's hermit crab and found it hours later in the washing machine (still kicking and much cleaner). All three angels put as much effort as possible into not getting along. Yes, I had had enough. And it was only 10 A.M.

Completely stressed, I picked up the phone and did the most logical thing—I called my sister. Was I looking for easy answers and words of wisdom? No. I was looking for something only another mom could give: understanding and support. You see, I knew that Charlene was most likely having a very similar day. And sometimes just knowing you're not alone makes all the difference.

We have a lot of resources available to us Christians. We can walk into any Christian bookstore and obtain countless books on prayer, marriage, or child rearing. But sometimes we overlook one of the most important resources that the Lord has given us: each other.

Friendships are truly one of God's greatest gifts, and He provides these special relationships for different aspects of our lives. Erelene is a mentor as we share our faith, writing, and poetry. Holly and I share a love for music and Christian drama, as well as the challenges of parenthood. We can talk for hours about nothing—and everything. Debbie and I have been friends for years. We're raising our children together, worshipping together, growing together. Jan and I became very close for a season, as we worked with one heart and mind on a summer mission trip. She continues to be an example to me of godly living. Our ladies' group at church meets monthly to serve and to pray for missions. We also serve and pray for each other as we share trials and triumphs.

God wants us to enjoy the fellowship of

other believers. He gave us as gifts to each other to love, share, support, and encourage.

What wonderful gifts!

◦◦◦

Oh Father,
thank You for the
beautiful gifts of friendship
You have given me.
My friends touch my life
in so many ways.
Show me how to love,
encourage, build up,
and support those around me,
that I may guide them
closer to You.

◦◦◦

Two are better than one. . . . If one falls down, his friend can help him up.

ECCLESIASTES 4:9–10

JUST A NICKEL

*He will be a joy
and delight to you,
and many will rejoice
because of his birth.*

LUKE 1:14

If I had a dollar for every time I've wanted to resign this job of motherhood, I would be incredibly wealthy. I could hire around-the-clock maids and nannies to take care of all the tedious little details. Then I would be free to leisurely sip my Diet Mountain Dew while I watched reruns of *Little House on the Prairie*. I might even loan out a nanny or two to friends so that we could meet and "do lunch" at quaint little restaurants and browse in fashionable boutiques.

If I had a quarter for every time I've wanted to open a window and toss out a child (or two or three), I would be so rich I could take exotic vacations around the world. I might even purchase my own yacht and explore uncharted waters. Countries would come to me for a loan—and I might even consider getting this one out of debt.

But if I had *just a nickel* for every time I've kissed a cheek or sweet baby feet; or every time a little smile has carried me through a day; or my heart has pounded and I caught my breath over my love for them—well then perhaps the whole world could not hold the riches I would have.

Lord,
thank You for the wealth of love
and joy you have given me.
Thank You for revealing
to my heart the preciousness of
this time in my life.

"For where your treasure is, there your heart will be also." MATTHEW 6:21

Glorifying Him

Ascribe to the Lord
the glory due his name.
Bring an offering
and come before him;
worship the LORD in
the splendor of his holiness.

1 CHRONICLES 16:29

Yesterday, our drama team performed in front of several hundred people. The staging was good and the lighting was perfect. Soft music provided a moving backdrop to the gospel message. Onstage, our timing was great, evidence of the prayer-cover requested minutes earlier. Afterward, we met and fellowshipped with the audience. We heard testimony of hearts and lives touched. We heard God praised because of our words. Our hearts beat wildly and tears came easily as we praised God for the opportunity to glorify Him.

Today, I wipe runny noses, change diapers, and settle arguments. I wash endless piles of laundry, grade homework, and prepare meals. The staging is our semi-clean home, the lighting is a florescent bulb that needs dusting. Background music is a two-year-old singing "Old MacDonald" at the top of her lungs. I pause just a moment and reflect on the previous day. What a joy it was to glorify God!

Then I feel a gentle but persistent tug. Katie's baby eyes gaze longingly into mine. "Finger hurt, Mama, kiss it!" Instantly, I kneel and bring my face to hers, kissing her forehead. Then, because she's not quite sure just which finger she hurt, I kiss each one in turn. After a hug, I send a much happier baby on her way.

As she toddles away, I become aware of my pounding heart and watering eyes. Yes, yesterday the Lord was glorified through drama. But today, He was glorified through a most precious and unique way: a mother's touch.

Oh Father,
what joy to serve You
by being a mother!
Open my eyes to the
sacredness of this calling.
I pray for strength and guidance
that I may walk worthy of
the name of mother.

Then Hannah prayed and said: "My heart rejoices in the LORD; in the LORD my horn is lifted high. My mouth boasts over my enemies, for I delight in your deliverance. There is no one holy like the LORD; there is no one besides you; there is no Rock like our God.

1 SAMUEL 2:1–2

SIDETRACKED

She sets about her work vigorously;
her arms are strong for her tasks.

PROVERBS 31:17

The other day I woke up early with an incredible sense of purpose. *Today,* I thought, *I'm going to make something happen. I'm going to delight my husband and bring a smile to his face. I'm going to clean out our bedroom closet.*

Immediately after breakfast, I marched directly to my chosen project. "Daddy won't even recognize the place when I get through," I proudly announced to my girls. I opened the closet door with a grimace. What used to be a walk-in model had slowly become a step-in-carefully model. Kicking shoes and a fallen jacket aside, I cleared enough space to sit comfortably and looked around. *What's one of Katie's diapers and that Barbie doll head doing in here?* While I returned the items to Katie's room, I noticed her unmade bed and the cookie crumbs in the carpet. I quickly tidied the bed and went for the vacuum.

The closet where I keep the vacuum also houses old videotapes. *Ooh*, I thought, *I haven't watched that one in a long time.* As I put the video on the television to watch later, I noticed crayon marks on the TV screen. While I grabbed the cleaning spray from over the kitchen sink, I found, to my delight, that pretty Christmas candle I had searched for months ago. I went back to the living room with the cleaning spray and the candle in my hand.

The girls, however, intercepted me halfway. "We wanna snack, Mom."

"That sounds good," I said. "How about some chocolate chip cookies? Hey, and we can watch an old video I found!"

Later that evening, Roy asked about my day. To my chagrin I realized I had accomplished little more than moving a few items from one place to another. I had started several projects, but I hadn't completed anything.

Tomorrow, however, will be different. I am going to tackle that hall closet and re-arrange all those videos. I wonder what's in there anyway. . . .

Lord,
I need Your help.
Forgive me for wasted time.
Help me to commit myself to
what I begin so that I may
be a better example to my children.

Be very careful, then, how you live—not as unwise but as wise, making the most of every opportunity.   EPHESIANS 5:15–16

THROUGH
LITTLE EYES

*From the lips of
children and infants
you have ordained praise.*

PSALM 8:2

Before each child entered the crawl-around, get-into-everything stage, I would crawl around on all fours myself in order to "childproof" our home. It was a great way to gain perspective into their little world and to see things on their level. But as the girls have grown, I've realized that babyhood isn't the only time that it's important to look through a child's eyes.

Sometimes, we moms are so busy training, instructing, and sharing our bits of wisdom, we forget that our children have quite a lot to teach us—if we'll take the time to learn. Their fresh, innocent way of viewing the world reminds us to enjoy the little moments. And quite often what seems ordinary to us becomes spectacular from a child's perspective.

My friend Holly and her daughter were admiring a full moon when Mary Cate announced with three-year-old wonder, "Look, Mama, the moon has all its pieces!" With a smile and a hug, the moment was sealed in that mother's heart for all time.

Children remind us to laugh, no—giggle. They encourage us to put the lawn chair away and to run, jump, skip, twirl, and maybe even try a cartwheel or two. They help us rediscover the simple joys of the sun on our face and grass under bare feet.

But even more important, children teach us about God. They prove that little bodies can have big faith. They show us how to pray believing and how to live abundantly. They take their Heavenly Father at His word, and they expect us to do the same.

What happiness God must feel when His little messengers reach the heart of an adult! For surely He is pleased when we remember to take joy in loving Him, in just being His child.

Lord,
what joy and wonder
You give me through the children!
Thank You for
wide eyes and innocent ways,
and for reminding me to
keep a childlike perspective on life.
Help me to always see
the spectacular in the
seemingly ordinary events of each day.

"I tell you the truth, anyone who will not receive the kingdom of God like a little child will never enter it."   MARK 10:15

TOO HEAVY

When I called,
you answered me;
you made me bold
and stouthearted.

PSALM 138:3

The hour is late. Wearily, I complete my bedtime routine and make my way down the hall for a last peek at the girls. I pause outside each door and listen to the steady breathing. On impulse, I enter Laura and Mary's room and tiptoe over to their bunk beds. *They're sleeping so peacefully, so angelically. Are these the same two little girls who fought over just about everything today?*

As I reach out and adjust Laura's covers, I remember that she wanted to talk about something earlier. *What was it?* She approached me several times, but I was too busy—fixing supper, phone calls, the baby had all taken precedence over her need to talk. With a sigh of regret, I kiss her softly and resolve to find a few minutes of one-on-one time with her tomorrow.

Mary has one arm flung over her head and one leg off the bed. Sweet, easy-going Mary. Sandwiched somewhere between a budding preteen and a toddler, I rarely have to worry about Mary. *Is that wise? Have I put my relationship with Mary on cruise control? Is she getting lost in the middle?*

In the adjacent room, little curls frame a sweet baby face. *This couldn't possibly be the tiny tyrant who emptied a container of baby powder in her room and turned over my potted plants today.* With a smile, I lean over and brush my lips against a chubby cheek. *Mommy will be more patient tomorrow, I promise.*

With a heart full of worries, concerns, and regrets, I make my way to my bedside and do the only logical thing. Like countless times before, the burdens of motherhood become too heavy for these frail shoulders—so I take them to Someone infinitely stronger. On my knees, I confess shortcomings and failures, fears and concerns. I acknowledge my weaknesses and inadequacies and lean on the ultimate Source of strength.

Oh what joy to know that I don't have to face tomorrow with my own strength! How wonderful to know that the ultimate power Source is on my side, ready to steady my faltering steps and pick me up in His loving arms when I fall. Praise God!

Oh thank You again, Father,
for the privilege of
coming to You in prayer.
Thank You for allowing me to
lay my burdens at Your feet.
I praise You, Lord,
for your listening heart,
steadying hand, and forgiving ways.

"So do not fear, for I am with you; do not be dismayed, for I am your God. I will strengthen you and help you; I will uphold you with my righteous right hand." ISAIAH 41:10

POLKA-DOT PACKAGES

Praise the LORD, O my soul; all my inmost being, praise his holy name. Praise the LORD, O my soul, and forget not all his benefits.

PSALM 103:1–2

It's hard to believe, but the holidays are finally over. Today we took down the tree, carefully laying each ornament in its waiting place for next year. Fallen needles mix with dried poinsettia leaves and bits of ribbon as I sweep up the debris created from weeks of celebration. After some semblance of order is restored, I give the girls permission to delve into new toys and craft kits. Before long, the tabletop is covered with glitter, markers, and paints, as my little inventors lose themselves in the joy of creating (and mess-making).

Alone in my room, I enjoy looking over the assortment of gifts I received from friends and family. Each one was given with thoughtfulness and generosity. My favorite gift, however, is one that I initially didn't recognize as being a gift—and it came in a polka-dotted package.

Ten days before Christmas, I was changing Katie's diaper when I noticed, to my complete horror, bright red dots popping out all over her little body. Oh no, it couldn't be, not now, not at Christmas! With a wail and a martyr's sigh, I scooped her up and ran to find Roy. The look on his face confirmed my suspicions: chicken pox.

My whining began immediately. Why, Lord, why now? I have parties to attend, gifts to purchase, goodies to bake. I have *plans*.

Evidently, the Lord did, too, and as usual, His plans were infinitely better than my own. My typical Christmas rush came to a screeching halt as my whole focus shifted to a tiny, itchy, two-year-old. My heart went out to my little invalid as she pitifully cried, "Hold me, Mama, I got chicken on my face!"

And hold her I did. Instead of spending hours fighting the crowds, Katie and I spent hours in the rocking chair. So while the world rushed on by, the Lord let me experience a bit of Christmas I may have otherwise missed. As I rocked my little one, my thoughts drifted to that first

Christmas so long ago. The beautiful simplicity of how it must have been—a mother, a father, a baby—filled my heart with thanksgiving.

There will be other parties and other plans to make. But for now, for this moment in time, a polka-dotted toddler needs her mama, because. . . well, like she said, she has "chicken" on her face.

⟋⟍

Thank You, Father,
for reaching in with Your infinite
wisdom and slowing down my
frantic pace. Thank You for restoring
the lost simplicity in my life.
And thank You for the opportunity to
provide comfort to one of Your little ones.

⟋⟍

My heart is not proud, O LORD, my eyes are not haughty; I do not concern myself with great matters or things too wonderful for me. But I have stilled and quieted my soul.

PSALM 131:1–2

I RESOLVE

He will be the sure
foundation for your times,
a rich store of salvation
and wisdom and knowledge;
the fear of the Lord is
the key to this treasure.

ISAIAH 33:6

It's hard to believe, but we are standing on the threshold of a brand new year. Looking back, I can't help but wonder, *Where did last year go?* With excitement and anticipation I draw a deep breath and boldly take a first step into the future. I don't get very far, however, before I'm interrupted with that age-old, most irritating question: "So, what's your New Year's resolution?"

Oh good grief. Can't I just be happy about a new year without having to resolve something? Okay, I'll play along. I resolve. . .I resolve. . .I resolve to be more decisive. . .I guess. Well, I'll try anyway. And I'll clean out the refrigerator more often. Although personally, I think the moldy stuff in the back is very educational for the girls.

I'll try to remember to open the damper before I build a fire. I promise never, ever again to accidentally wash my red sweatshirt along with everyone's underwear. And I resolve most solemnly to never again use Roy's pliers to nail something on the wall (unless I can't find the hammer).

I'll try not to use the instant cash machine quite so often (unless I run out of checks). Oh, and I'll do better about recording in the check register the checks I do write. And I'll definitely put a stop to my impulse buying—unless, of course, it's on sale, wherein I declare the previous resolution null and void.

Wow. That's a lot of changes to make in one year. Maybe I should just concentrate on one or two. . . .

Father,
I want to thank You for
the blessings of the past year.
You have been at work
in my life in countless ways.
I praise You for Your faithfulness
and especially for Your forgiveness.
As I begin a new year,
remind me to grow from
my mistakes and to give
every moment to You.

It is good to praise the LORD and make music to your name, O Most High, to proclaim your love in the morning and your faithfulness at night. PSALM 92:1–2

UNEXPECTED GIFTS

*This is the day
the LORD has made;
let us rejoice and be glad in it.*

PSALM 118:24

God's abiding love is all around us. Our children, family, our home, our daily bread, all speak volumes about the Master's care for us. Sometimes, however, I am completely overwhelmed by one of His unexpected love gifts.

It may take the form of a surprise friendship, drawing close to someone with whom I never expected to have anything in common. Or it may show up as an unusual opportunity or a unique area of service—something I know is only possible through Christ.

The girls and I received one of those surprise gifts one unseasonably warm day in January. The preceding weeks had been typically cold and rainy. We had even experienced some southern sleet and a few white flakes of something called "snow." Inside, we were all experiencing that after-holiday lull, and our tempers were short as the days turned into weeks without fresh air and sunshine.

Then it happened. God sent us three consecutive days of beautiful spring weather—smack dab in the middle of winter. Oh, it was wonderful! I opened the front door and set the captives free! We ran, we rode bikes, we picnicked, we savored every moment of those three awesome days.

Of course the cold did return, but it settled around a much happier family. Our short reprieve from winter's fury stayed in our hearts over the long weeks ahead. What a thoughtful gift!

Father,
what joy You give us
through unexpected pleasures!
Thank You for
the beauty of Your creation
and for opportunities to enjoy it.
And thank You for
the many times You offer glimpses of
spring in the winters of my life.

Your love, O LORD, reaches to the heavens, your
faithfulness to the skies.   PSALM 36:5

DATE NIGHT

*A wife of noble character is
her husband's crown,
but a disgraceful wife is
like decay in his bones.*

PROVERBS 12:4

Tonight is a special night. The sitter is all lined up, and Roy and I are going out on a date. I can't wait. I've been daydreaming about it for hours. I dreamily picture a secluded table for two, soft lighting, and our favorite Chinese food buffet.

Tonight, I vow, I'm going to be especially attentive. Out of all the men in the world, God gave this one to me. I'm going to look him in the eyes and hang on his every word. Yes, after this dinner, he'll know just how much he's loved and appreciated.

As soon as we're seated and served, I lean close and say, "Tell me about your day, honey." Then I settle back with eagerness and adoration written all over my face, while I listen to him talk.

Now, I am a creative, artsy kind of person. If you start throwing numbers, equations, and various types of logical stuff my way, it's like tossing me into a pile of quicksand. No matter how hard I try to hang on and concentrate, I invariably sink.

Roy, on the other hand, is Mr. Logical himself. He thrives on megabytes, ROM, and ram (don't ask). He has computer chips for a late-night snack. When we recently received an electronic dartboard as a gift, I agonized over where it would look best in the house; Roy wanted to take it apart and analyze its internal organs. Get the picture?

So now I take a bite of egg roll and gaze lovingly across the table. I'm doing pretty well so far; I understand he just upgraded our modem from 14.4k to 56k. After a few minutes, however, I inevitably drift off, lost somewhere between "chips" and "extended memory." My eyes are still fixed on his, but I'm thinking about how I love the color of his hair and how I could become lost in those expressive blue eyes of his.

Of course panic seeps in when I realize that Roy has stopped talking and has a question in his eyes. *Oh, what was he saying?* Cleverly I cover with, "That's great, honey, want some more fried rice?" (I don't think he noticed that he lost me—although those expressive blue eyes do look a tad exasperated.)

Father,
thank You once again for my husband.
Help me to recognize and appreciate
his unique gifts and abilities.
And as we share our lives together,
may I always be a source of
support and encouragement.

The Lord God said, "It is not good for the man to be alone. I will make a helper suitable for him."   GENESIS 2:18

EXPECTATIONS

Better a little with
the fear of the LORD than
great wealth with turmoil.

PROVERBS 15:16

Driving along the North Carolina coastline, we could hardly contain our excitement as we attempted to locate the cottage reserved for our summer vacation. Although it was still early May, we were getting an unexpected sneak preview of our home-for-a-week in the summer. The entire family had just enjoyed an evangelism conference at Fort Caswell, North Carolina, and we had decided to run over and check out the lodging arrangements we had seen only in a small black-and-white photo. Saving and planning for the big week was a united family project, so everyone was equally enthusiastic.

As we neared the general area of the cottage, Roy slowed the truck so the girls could focus on the addresses. I was the first to squeal, "I see it!" This was to be our first time going to the beach for an entire week, and I had already begun daydreaming about the wonder of staying in a castle by the sea. Of course, ours was to be second-row, but that was okay; we were still thrilled!

But as we pulled into the small, rutted driveway, my heart sank as I stared up at our not-so-grand future lodgings. Peeling paint and a questionable roof screamed for a good dose of tender loving care. The cottage certainly didn't look as if it could handle the shenanigans of an exuberant family of five.

With a sigh, I agreed to walk across the street with Laura and Mary to say "hello" and "good-bye" to the ocean. Slowly, I turned back for another glimpse of the cottage, irrationally hoping that perhaps it had spruced itself up while I wasn't looking.

"Well, girls," I said, trying to sound positive, "what do you think?"

Almost in unison and with awe in their voices, they exclaimed, "Oh, Mama, it's beautiful!"

Surprised, I stood and followed their gaze—but this time I looked through little-girl eyes. Instead of focusing on peeling paint, I envisioned three swimsuit-clad bodies eagerly awaiting Mom and Dad on the upper deck. I saw wide eyes and little hands as they offered up beach treasures for parental inspection. Instead of inconvenience, I saw fun, laughter, and memories.

I didn't lower my expectations; I raised them to what is really important: time together as a family, making memories for a lifetime.

Father,
thank You for speaking through
my children to remind me of
what is truly important.
Thank You for the opportunity to
experience life through children's eyes.

LORD, you have assigned me my portion and my cup; you have made my lot secure. The boundary lines have fallen for me in pleasant places; surely I have a delightful inheritance.   PSALM 16:5–6

WITH MY WHOLE HEART

*Cast all your anxiety on him
because he cares for you.*

1 PETER 5:7

The sun streams brilliantly through our dining area windows. Absently acknowledging the warmth on my face, I stare blankly, not focusing on anything in particular. Somehow, the sun's heat fails to penetrate to my heart; I feel cold and detached from my pleasant surroundings. Throughout the day, I try to respond to the girls' good-natured antics, but my smile never reaches my eyes. Tired and emotionally drained, I attempt a rational review of the last few weeks.

God's call had been so strong in our lives. Roy and I had felt deeply a command to follow Christ in an unexpected way. A crisis in our belief followed, leading to time on our knees seeking God's heart. Hearts and wills were broken, and life-changing decisions were made.

The peace that followed was all encompassing. Although difficult and painful, the decision left us unquestionably in the center of God's will.

As the days slipped by, however, I allowed doubts to begin seeping in; I gave Satan a foothold in my thoughts. I began questioning our thought processes, and our initial peace and joy was replaced with confusion and uncertainty.

Now I continued to stare anxiously out into the bareness of a winter that reflected the condition of my heart. Even prayer seemed impossible; I couldn't find the words to express my inner turmoil.

Finally, in desperation, I searched the Scriptures once again, aching for divine direction. *Please, Lord,* I cried, *help me pray. . . .* And then there, nestled in the book of Romans, was the beautiful comfort and direction I had been seeking. Hungrily, I read, "the Spirit helps us in our weakness. We do not know what we ought to pray for, but the Spirit himself intercedes for us with groans that words cannot express" (8:26).

I sank to my knees and wept. Without

making a sound, I raised my hands in prayer and praise. I cried out to the Spirit with my whole heart, asking Him to seek the Father's face on my behalf.

Almost immediately, the clarity and certainty of God's plan returned and banished my anxious thoughts. Springtime replaced the bleakness in my soul, and I fellowshipped once more with my Master.

Oh, how God responds to the hurting, seeking heart!

Oh Father,
sometimes my heart is
so burdened that I seem
unable to reach You.
Nothing I do succeeds in piercing
the darkness around me.
But Father, how I praise You for
revealing through Your Word that
it's not up to me to reach You.
When I humbly and
fervently seek Your face,
Your love and comfort surround me
and drive away all doubt and fear.
Thank You, dear Lord!

Seek the LORD while he may be found; call on him while he is near. ISAIAH 55:6

THE JOY
TO COME

Surely goodness and love
will follow me
all the days of my life,
and I will dwell in the house
of the LORD forever.

PSALM 23:6

The Christian life is definitely not an easy one. We face countless hardships, trials, and temptations. We juggle the demands of family, career, and church responsibilities. We fret about health and finances. We grieve over the loss of loved ones. All too easily, we become weary and disillusioned as we question our hope and purpose.

When daily burdens become overwhelming, I love to read Paul's second letter to the Corinthians. He reminds them not to lose heart when they have trials and persecutions. He encourages his fellow believers to fix their eyes on Jesus instead of the things of this world. Our troubles, he says, are "light and momentary" compared to the eternal glories to come.

As a mom, I need to take time to set aside worldly cares and focus on eternal joys. I like to envision the beautiful reunions in store for the believer. Wives will be reunited with husbands. Parents will joyfully embrace their children. Mothers will tenderly cradle little ones that were lost to them on earth. And we will all meet at Jesus' feet, our hungry eyes feasting on His awesome and precious face.

How wonderful to know that in Christ we have a solid hope and future! How comforting that at this very moment, Jesus is preparing eternity for us. And how awesome that our Creator actually wants us to spend forever in His presence. Oh, what joy waits for us!

Precious Lord,
how I delight in knowing that
I'll be spending eternity with You!
Thank You for
Your promise of eternal life.
Thank You for putting
my earthly troubles into
heavenly perspective.

Therefore we do not lose heart. Though outwardly we are wasting away, yet inwardly we are being renewed day by day. For our light and momentary troubles are achieving for us an eternal glory that far outweighs them all. So we fix our eyes not on what is seen, but on what is unseen. For what is seen is temporary, but what is unseen is eternal.

2 CORINTHIANS 4:16–18

WHAT'S COOKIN'?

I delight in your decrees;
I will not neglect your word.

PSALM 119:16

I'm not quite sure how it happened, but in the first years of our marriage, I got the reputation for not being very adept in the kitchen. Sure, I made some mistakes. But hasn't everyone? I mean, to my knowledge I've never actually poisoned anyone.

Of course there was the time I prepared a fondue dinner for several friends. Concerned about the beef being tough, I used half a bottle of tenderizer. Oh, the meat was incredibly tender—but everyone had to down a glass of water between bites to keep from choking on the salty flavor.

I also have to admit I didn't drain the grease off the hamburger the first time I made tacos; everyone got an upset stomach that time. But that's an honest mistake, don't you think?

And over time I have improved. Of course,

just when I begin feeling like Betty Crocker herself, one of the girls will bring me back to reality with, "Mom, are we having the pork chops that you chew a long time?" When they see my stricken face, they usually come back with, "It's okay, Mom, I like 'em like that— really."

It's not that I don't like to cook. I just get impatient with all the little details. I mean, if the recipe calls for only a teaspoon of something, is it really that important? And must I actually mix the batter for three minutes, when it looks fine to me after a minute and a half?

Oh well, maybe I'm not completely hopeless. After all, my sister taught me how to make homemade bread from starter. Starter—wow. It even sounds impressive. I have starter in my fridge. Of course Charlene explained to me that I have to "feed" it every eight or nine days. Uh-oh. This is beginning to sound complicated. I wonder if it would eat the leftover spaghetti from last Tuesday. . . .

Father,
help me to remember the old adage,
"If it's worth doing,
it's worth doing right."
Especially, Lord,
when it comes to my time with You.
Remind me to not take shortcuts when I
read and meditate on Your Word.
And thank You, Father,
for turning my many blunders
into something beautiful for You.

But his delight is in the law of the LORD, and
on his law he meditates day and night.

PSALM 1:2

NO SENSE OF LOYALTY

Do not offer the parts of
your body to sin,
as instruments of wickedness,
but rather offer yourselves to God.

ROMANS 6:13

I hate my bathroom scale. It has no sense of loyalty whatsoever. I mean, all I did was overeat just a teensy bit last weekend, and it actually turned on me, claiming I had gained four pounds in three days. That's gratitude for you. I bought the scale in good faith. I placed it in a prominent place in the bathroom. I regularly replace the batteries to ensure complete accuracy. And now, with no warning at all, it mockingly flashes extra poundage at me.

The scale is obviously mistaken. I admit to savoring three pieces of my mom-in-law's world-famous chocolate pie—but I was standing up when I ate them. And we all know those calories don't count. I also sneaked a few items off Roy's tray when we went out Saturday night. But it's common knowledge that food originating from someone else's plate is completely void of calories or fat grams. And yes, I confess to inhaling a half-dozen doughnuts in one sitting. But that was only because I feared recrimination for leaving just two or three in the box. I had to eat them all in order to destroy the evidence that they ever existed in the first place.

So you see, the scale's claims are completely unfounded and irresponsible. But just as a precautionary measure, I plan to limit my snacking this week to low-cal popcorn. To help the taste, however, I'll need to use just a teensy-weensy bit of butter. . . .

Father,
sometimes my lack of
discipline amazes even me.
Help me to give everything to You,
including my eating habits.
I want to glorify You in all things.

Do not join those who drink too much wine or gorge themselves on meat, for drunkards and gluttons become poor, and drowsiness clothes them in rags.   PROVERBS 23:20–21

HE UNDERSTANDS

*. . .who forgives all your sins
and heals all your diseases.*

PSALM 103:3

It's a cold, wet morning in January. I'm sitting in the office of an oral surgeon where Laura is having five teeth removed in preparation for braces. Earlier, the surgeon suggested that it was best if Mom went to the waiting room, and reluctantly, I agreed. It's never easy seeing someone you love in a vulnerable position.

A tear escapes Laura's anxious eyes as I rise to leave. "It's okay, baby, everything will be okay." Bravely she nods and attempts a smile. *Be with her, Lord. Let her feel Your strength and presence.*

Prayerfully waiting, I think back to other times my heart has ached for my little ones. With Mary, severe croup sent us on a 2 A.M. trip to the hospital. I anxiously watched over her hospital crib, waiting for each breath. The five days of treatment seemed interminable.

I remember stitches and a broken bone. I call to mind pneumonia, mono, high fevers, and chicken pox. *Childhood isn't easy, is it, Lord?* And there is probably more pain to come. *Oh Father, I hate to see them hurt.*

As I continue to wait for Laura, I draw strength from knowing that the Lord understands exactly how I feel. He, too, hurts for His children. And not only for our physical pain; God is also grieved when we hurt spiritually and emotionally, especially when our hurt stems from sins of willfulness and disobedience.

How comforting that just as we can pray for physical healing, we can also pray for spiritual restoration. And how marvelous that God eagerly continues to offer His forgiving heart and healing hands. Hallelujah!

Father,
I am so glad that I am not alone
when I hurt for my children.
You also long for their physical
and spiritual well-being.
Show me how to lay
my concerns for them at Your feet.
I lift them up to You, Father.

Dear friend, I pray that you may enjoy good health and that all may go well with you, even as your soul is getting along well.   3 JOHN 2

BE STILL

Be still before the LORD
and wait patiently for him.

PSALM 37:7

"Let's get going, girls. We have a lot to do today. Katie honey, find your shoes for Mama. Mary, get the hairbrush. . . . Laura, that headband doesn't match your shirt. What's taking you all so long? It's time to go. . .now!"

Lord, where are You?

"Sure, I can help. What time do I need to be there? Do I need to bring anything? Four dozen cupcakes? Um. . .okay."

Lord, where are You?

"Honey, if I can get a sitter, we can catch the late movie tonight. Well, it has to be tonight; it's the only one we have free for the next two weeks."

Lord, where are You?

"Mary, where's your ball uniform? I need to get it washed if you're going to play tomorrow. Laura, your orthodontist appointment is in fifteen minutes, are you ready? Has anyone seen my watch? I left it right here."

Lord, please, where are You?

"Well, I'm already serving on three committees, but if you really need me, I guess I can. . ."

Oh Lord. . .are You there?

Be still, My child.
Be still and know that I am God.

Lord,
forgive me for falling
into such a hectic pace that
I fail to hear Your voice.
Help me to slow down,
Father. Teach me to truly
be still in Your presence
so that each and every day
I will have an awareness of
Your majesty and power.

"Be still before the LORD, all mankind, because
he has roused himself from his holy dwelling."
ZECHARIAH 2:13

THE DILEMMA

The mind of sinful man is death,
but the mind controlled by
the Spirit is life and peace.

ROMANS 8:6

When I get to heaven, one of the first things I'd like to do is to sit down with the Apostle Paul and have a nice long chat. The more I read about him, the more I like him. He seems so real, so human. I mean, he still struggled with worldly matters, even though he led an amazing life for the Lord.

In Romans 7, he shares his battle with his sinful nature: "For I have the desire to do what is good, but I cannot carry it out. For what I do is not the good I want to do; no, the evil I do not want to do—this I keep on doing" (18–19).

Mercy, I can really relate. As soon as I resolve to be more patient with the girls, I lose my temper and end up regretting things I said. And the moment I promise not to harp on the little things, I'll find an empty milk container in the fridge and lose complete control. I want to do the right thing, but my self seems to get in the way. The result? A conflict, a quandary, a dilemma. Is there an answer? Is there hope?

According to Paul, the solution centers on our mindset: whether we focus on our sinful nature or on what we know the Spirit desires. When Christ died for us, He set us free from sin and death, so we don't have to succumb to sin's destruction. Through Jesus' death and resurrection, we have victory over sin! We should fix our eyes on that spiritual truth rather than on our own human imperfection. When we do, we'll find the power available to us through Jesus. What a comfort to know we are not alone when we face life's inevitable dilemmas.

Father,
sometimes the harder I try,
the more I seem to fail.
Help me to put my trust solely in You,
that I may lead a Spirit-filled life.

You, however, are controlled not by the sinful nature but by the Spirit, if the Spirit of God lives in you. ROMANS 8:9

TOTALLY UNIQUE

*For God's gifts and
his call are irrevocable.*

ROMANS 11:29

I've had a very interesting day. Five little girls have been in my house: my three, plus Anna, my niece, and Caleigh, one of Katie's little friends. Counting me, that's six female personalities under one roof. Yes, it's been a very interesting day.

Throughout the morning the challenge has been to get everyone to agree on any one activity. So to my delight, my suggestion of going out for lunch was greeted with great enthusiasm. I chose a place that offers an indoor play area, and now, while my five bundles of energy run free, I sit back with a soft drink and a smile.

As I watch the girls play and interact with each other, I am fascinated by the five distinct personalities. From their physical characteristics to their temperaments, each child is wonderfully unique.

Laura is quiet, reflective, and creative. She likes to surprise those she loves with home-made cards and gifts. She'll dutifully perform any given task, but if you want to see fire in her eyes, you just have to step back and give her creative freedom.

Mary likes to run, jump, skip, and twirl. She wants to play longer, try harder, and go faster. But she also has an amazing spirit of discernment. Her tender heart goes out to anyone or anything she suspects may be suffering.

Little Caleigh is a true southern belle with a drawl that can melt any heart. With bright blue eyes and shy quiet ways, she is surprisingly friendly and open to those she's never met, especially senior adults.

Anna, or Annabelle as Aunt Leigh Ann calls her, has a genuine love and concern for God's tiny creatures. Her heart is open to things most of us overlook: frogs, caterpillars, moths, and butterflies. Best of all, though, she understands that God gave her this love for His creation. And she truly desires to please Him.

And then there's Katie. Her first words in the morning are, "Good mornin', Mama, I had a good nap!" She sings loud, hugs tight, and bounces just about everywhere she goes. If she's not tired, sick, or hungry, she's all smiles and sunshine.

Oh the joy God must take in the variety of His creations! How He must love to watch us live, grow, and learn. And how He must thrill to see us use our uniqueness for His glory.

Father,
I'm so excited to see the children's
unique strengths begin to shine through.
Guide me as I seek to encourage and
motivate them. May they use their gifts
for Your kingdom.

For this reason I remind you to fan into flame the gift of God, which is in you through the laying on of my hands.   2 TIMOTHY 1:6

I'M SORRY

A wise man's heart guides his mouth,
and his lips promote instruction.

PROVERBS 16:23

It was such a small thing. A minor childhood offense: a dropped toy, dropped repeatedly on bare floors. The sound echoed mercilessly through my aching head.

I quickly turned and in one unthinking moment brought pools of pain to sorrowful blue-green eyes. Trembling lips said haltingly, "I'm sorry, Mama."

More angry words rose inside me. I was tired. I'd had a long day. The aspirin I had taken earlier wasn't working. But as my eyes met hers, any defense of my thoughtlessness died on my lips. The Lord revealed to my heart that I could not excuse my cutting words to this little one He had entrusted to me.

Immediately, I pulled her into my arms, this beautiful, trusting, fragile gift from God. "No, honey, I'm sorry. Will you forgive me?"

There, in her precious, upturned face, could I possibly have glimpsed a deeper love and devotion?

How simple are the words "I'm sorry." But how difficult they can be to say. As a mom, I find myself anxious to justify any and all actions on my part, because, well, I'm the mom. But I'd be making an even bigger mistake if I didn't admit my shortcomings to the girls. They need to understand that no one is perfect, even parents, and that everyone is accountable for their actions.

"I'm sorry" makes Mom and Dad real, human, and accessible. And it fosters a priceless atmosphere of intimacy and trust.

Father,
too often I forget that moms
need to say "I'm sorry."
Forgive me when a prideful attitude
prevents me from being totally honest
with my children.
Remind me often that
my actions affect
impressionable little lives.

I have hidden your word in my heart that I might not sin against you.　　PSALM 119:11

THAT PESKY PLANK

"You hypocrite, first take the plank
out of your own eye, and then you will see clearly
to remove the speck from your brother's eye."

MATTHEW 7:5

I had had an aggravating day, and I was fuming. . . .

I can't believe it. I've waited by this phone all afternoon and they didn't call. Don't they realize that I have other things to do than sit by the phone? They said they would call. I guess some people just have no sense of responsibility.

"The check's in the mail." Yeah, right. I've been there, heard that. The mail hasn't been this slow since the Pony Express.

"I'll be there first thing in the morning." Uh huh. It's been three days, and Mr. First Thing hasn't shown yet with his work estimate. Does he think that my life revolves around waiting on him? Is his *business so good that he doesn't need mine?*

"Girls, I told you to clean out from under your beds."

"But, Mama. . ."

"Don't 'but, Mama' me. I don't want anything left under those beds!"

Later that evening as I was preparing supper and muttering under my breath at the same time, Roy asked, "Rough day, honey?"

Pitifully, I poured out the details of my day. "Why can't people just do what they say they're going to do?" I wailed.

"I don't know, honey. By the way, did you set up that doctor's appointment for me?"

"Uh. . .doctor's appointment?"

"Yes, doctor's appointment. And I received a second notice from your book club. Didn't you mail that check I gave you?"

"Um. . ." (I was beginning to squirm.)

"And the girls told me you wanted them to clean out from under their beds."

"That's right," I offered defensively.

"Well, they want to know why there's stuff under our bed."

"That's different, I'm storing things."

"Uh huh." His smirk was extremely irritating.

(Big sigh.) Does anybody have a crowbar I can borrow? I have a pesky plank to pry loose from my eye. . . .

Dear Lord,
why is it so easy to see the faults
and inconsistencies of others. . .
and yet be so blind to my own?
Please forgive me for judging others
when I too am so much at fault.
Give me a spirit of patience,
understanding, and forgiveness
as I strive to make every thought
and action a reflection of You.

If we confess our sins, he is faithful and just and will forgive us our sins and purify us from all unrighteousness.   1 JOHN 1:9

GIFT OF PRAYER

*The prayer of a righteous man
is powerful and effective.*

JAMES 5:16

I love to display family photos. From the professionally made to the simplest snapshot, our home is littered with captured family moments. My favorites are the girls in natural, unposed shots, like playing on the beach, hanging upside down on the swing set, or fishing with Dad. Rich with memories, each precious photo tells its own unique story.

I also enjoy old photos. I am fascinated by faded black-and-white pictures of my parents and grandparents in the child-rearing years of their lives. Those photos remind me that my parents and grandparents were where I am—and they actually survived it. Yes!

Two of my favorite black-and-whites, however, are of small children. One is a boy about four years old, who is wearing a jacket, tie, and the most adorable grin; the other is a baby girl with chubby cheeks and curling hair: Roy and me when we were small. Recently, as I walked past the photos where they hang on our wall, I stopped short and the thought hit me: *Who would have ever dreamed that these two children would grow up, fall in love, and marry?* I touched Roy's boyhood picture and thanked God for His infinite goodness.

Then it really hit me. Somewhere, in some other moms' living rooms, are cherished photos of three little boys. . .who will grow up, fall in love with my girls, and ask to marry them! Wow. *But, Lord,* I breathed, *are they being raised in Your Word? Are they being taught about You and Your goodness? Are You the head of their homes?*

As I began to pray, my eyes were opened to the opportunity before me. I realized I had the privilege and responsibility to pray for my girls' future spouses. Through my prayers I could touch the future homes of my children. The wonder of it is truly amazing. What a tremendous gift God has entrusted to parents!

Father,
thank You for the privilege of
interceding on behalf of my children.
I place them in Your hands, Lord.
And, Father,
I pray for the young men who
will someday desire a relationship
with our girls.
Please keep them strong
and true for You.

"If you remain in me and my words remain in you, ask whatever you wish, and it will be given to you."   JOHN 15:7

ORGANIZATION
(OR LACK THEREOF)

*But everything should be done
in a fitting and orderly way.*

1 CORINTHIANS 14:40

Roy made the most outrageous statement the other day. "Honey," he said, "you really need to be more organized."

"Why, whatever do you mean, my dear?"

"You know exactly what I mean. Take your desk, for example. I don't see how in the world you keep track of anything—it's completely covered."

"I know precisely where everything is," I countered. "Each and every stack of stuff has its own unique purpose. Besides, a messy desk is a sign of intelligence and creativity. Everybody knows that."

"Oh?" he said condescendingly. "Then what about the junk drawer?"

"Which one?" I ground out.

"My point exactly."

"Now wait just a minute. . . ." I definitely didn't like the way this conversation was going.

"And what about the top of the refrigerator?" he continued.

He was going too far now. "For goodness sakes, honey, no one can see up there unless they're over six feet tall."

"My point is, if you kept everything clutter free and in its place, you wouldn't spend so much time searching for lost items." He was beginning to make sense and that in itself was irritating me.

I finally relented. "Okay, starting next week I'll begin the declutter process."

He wasn't going to let me off that easily. "Why don't you just tackle something right now and be done with it?"

"Honey, I can't right this moment. I have some writing to do. By the way, have you seen my favorite pen? I left it here on my desk. . . ."

Oh Lord,
how much time have I wasted,
thrown away, lost. . .
just looking for that
illusive pen, set of keys,
or pair of sunglasses?
Create in me a desire for organization
and a spirit of discipline
that I may be a better steward
of every moment You have given me.

For though I am absent from you in body, I am present with you in spirit and delight to see how orderly you are and how firm your faith in Christ is. COLOSSIANS 2:5

Sunday Morning Chaos

*" 'These people honor me
with their lips,
but their hearts are far from me.' "*

MATTHEW 15:8

I plopped down in my chair at Sunday school with an incredible sense of triumph. I had made it. I was here! Pride oozed from my every pore.

The night before, I had made sure the girls were bathed and their heads washed. Then I checked the troops' Sunday wardrobes for dresses, shoes, stockings, bows, and clips. Satisfied that all was in order, I proceeded to my own room to sort, iron, and lay out my clothes for the next morning.

Now, over the years, experience has taught me that just because everything is lined up on Saturday night, that doesn't necessarily mean Sunday morning will go smoothly. I know for a fact that mischievous little angels (or demons) sneak into church-going homes and wreak havoc on a mother's hard work. Sunday mornings dawn with the inevitable missing shoe, hole in a stocking, or previously unnoticed stain on a child's clothing.

And sure enough, this morning was no exception. Laura was missing a button, Mary couldn't find the hairbrush, and Katie, well, she was being a normal two-year-old. Undaunted, however, I faced each situation head-on, and the Thomases arrived at church safely and on time.

As I sat in class basking in my accomplishment, the teacher asked if everyone had enjoyed reading the lesson as much as he had. Suddenly, panic washed over me as I realized that I had not even looked at this week's lesson. I couldn't even recall the Scripture references for the week. In fact, my body was in such a state of overdrive, I could barely shift gears into a listening and learning mode.

Talk about being under conviction! I had been spending so much time getting ready for church, I had neglected the most important preparation: spiritual readiness. I was putting more emphasis on my family's outward appearance than on our inner thoughts and attitudes. Potential joy in worship was being lost in Sunday morning chaos.

God used the experience as a serious wake-up call. . .and a lesson in humility. Once again, I praised Him and thanked Him for His forgiveness—and for His gentle reminder of what's truly important.

Lord,
help me to make spiritual preparation
for worship a priority.
May our greatest desire be to draw closer
to You so that our family may know
true joy in worship.

I rejoiced with those who said to me, "Let us go to the house of the Lord."　　PSALM 122:1

TIME OUT

After he had dismissed them,
he went up on a mountainside
by himself to pray.

MATTHEW 14:23

When the girls misbehave, their discipline can range from a swat on the rump, to losing a privilege, to being sent to their rooms for some "time out." But the more I think about the latter method, the more I question its effectiveness. I mean, really. I'm telling a child to go to a quiet place, alone, to ponder her actions. This is supposed to be punishment? Think about it: peace and quiet, solitude, and a chance to think. It sounds like heaven to me.

I wonder what I would need to do to be sent to my room. If I simply made a request for temporary exile, I know what would happen: My family would insist on knowing why and would all stand at the bedroom door demanding to know what I was doing. No, I need to get sent to my room.

Let's see, what if I threw a tantrum and refused to prepare dinner? No, they'd just cheer and order a pizza. What if I threw a tantrum, didn't bathe for a few days, and wore absolutely no makeup? Hmm. . .that might do it. Of course, then I might not want to be alone with myself.

Seriously, though, moms do need to take time out. Stepping away from our routine can be an invaluable way to catch our breath and gain perspective.

When I worked fulltime, my lunch hour was my catch-my-breath time. Whether running errands or eating with friends, I savored every moment of my downtime. Now that I'm at home, we have mandatory quiet time after lunch. I can read, write, or do absolutely nothing for a few precious minutes.

There's just something about being away from the children once in a while that makes me love and appreciate them all the more. Somehow, a few quiet moments have the power to refresh, revive, and restore. I come back to my family with new strength and energy for this awesome thing called motherhood.

Lord,
help me to remember the
importance of personal quiet time.
After all,
even in Your earthly ministry,
You withdrew to
spend time with the Father.
And, Lord,
remind me to use these moments wisely,
as a time to draw from
Your never-ending strength.

"Come with me by yourselves to a quiet place and get some rest." MARK 6:31

MISSION FIELD

" 'Speak, Lord,
for your servant is listening.' "

1 SAMUEL 3:9

I sat spellbound as the guest speaker shared experiences from her years of missionary service in Kenya. With a crown of white hair and clear blue eyes, this gentle servant's face seemed to glow with love for her Lord. I was moved to tears as story after story unfolded, demonstrating God's faithfulness to people in physical and spiritual poverty. As I listened, I found myself drawn to this servant of God in a way that seemed to reach to the very depths of my heart. Deeply moved, I fervently prayed, *Oh Lord, I want to serve You like that! I want to go. I want to do something for You. Oh Father, please show me my mission field!*

Later that week, lost in my regular routine, I found myself questioning my earlier feelings of urgency. *You know, Lord, where is my mission field? I have a husband and children. I have endless responsibilities. I can't just run off to a foreign country. I truly felt Your call to deeper servant-hood, but what is it You want me to do?*

I could almost hear the heavens sigh as the light went on in my mind and heart. *That's right, I am a wife and mother. My first calling is to serve God by serving my family.* I felt a thrill as I realized that I am a missionary, right here, right now. By divine appointment I am here in this place to minister to those with whom I come in contact. After her family, a mom's mission field includes neighbors, the check-out girl in the grocery store, the elderly lady sitting alone in the next booth at McDonald's, and anyone else the Lord lays on our hearts. God wants us to open our spiritual eyes and be aware of what He's already doing around us. All He asks is that we be willing, ready, and faithful to His call.

Father,
I am humbled by Your call on my life.
I stand amazed that You would
entrust me with
touching others in Your name.
May I be ever aware of
the tremendous privilege and
responsibility You have given me.
Open my eyes, Lord,
to every opportunity for service.

Always be prepared to give an answer to everyone who asks you to give the reason for the hope that you have. . . . For Christ died for sins once for all, the righteous for the unrighteous, to bring you to God.

1 PETER 3:15,18

ONE ON ONE

*Therefore encourage one another
and build each other up,
just as in fact you are doing.*

1 THESSALONIANS 5:11

Mary's birthday is fast approaching, and with typical seven-year-old enthusiasm, she has planned every detail. She knows where the party will be, who will be there, and what kind of cake we will serve. Not leaving anything to chance, she has officially counted down the days for the past two months. Each morning begins with something like, "Guess whose birthday is in forty-three days?"

One of her most anticipated events has been a one-on-one lunch and shopping trip with Mom. A fairly new tradition in our family, both Mom and daughters are always excited about spending time alone with each other.

Back in November, Laura and I spent a glorious day walking, talking, and clothes shopping. We teased and giggled like two schoolgirls and enjoyed each other as friends as well as mother and child. That was a priceless afternoon when I had the chance to see Laura as an individual, without the distractions of sibling rivalries, the television, or the telephone.

Today, as I sit at a table for two with my middle daughter, I am completely overwhelmed by how she's grown and changed over the past few months. *How long has it been since I've really looked into her eyes and hung on every word?* Not worried about interruptions from her sisters, Mary is visibly relaxed and very talkative. She shares her thoughts on everything from Beanie Babies, to growing up, to her future home in heaven. I am impressed by her wit and thought-provoking questions.

When I finally get a word in, I exclaim, "You know, Mary, you are the neatest, most fascinating eight-year-old I know! I'm so glad God gave you to me!"

She didn't have to say a word; her exuberant little face said it all. What a simple thing, to spend one-on-one time with the girls—but what awesome and eternal benefits!

Lord,
with all the
responsibilities of motherhood,
it sometimes seems impossible to
find time alone with each child.
Thank You for the privilege of
these rare and precious moments.
Help me to avoid waiting for
special occasions but to carve a
few moments out of each day to
acknowledge them as individuals.
And guide me, Father,
as I encourage each girl to
seek Your master plan for her life.

He took a little child and had him stand among them. Taking him in his arms, he said to them, "Whoever welcomes one of these little children in my name welcomes me; and whoever welcomes me does not welcome me but the one who sent me." MARK 9:36–37

BATTLE OF WILLS

*You know that the testing of
your faith develops perseverance.
Perseverance must finish its work so that you may
be mature and complete, not lacking anything.*

JAMES 1:3–4

Ladies and gentlemen, if I may direct your attention to the Thomas living room. . . . In one corner, at approximately five feet seven inches and weighing in at an undisclosed amount, we have a physically and mentally exhausted mom. Across the room, at just under three feet tall and a measly twenty-eight pounds, we have the defending world champion of mother-child mind games. So get your seats early, folks. This confrontation has been building for days. And it promises to be the matchup of the century. . . .

Yes, today has been one long battle of wills. One would think that by my third two-year-old I would have this stuff down pat. Not hardly. My little darling has done the exact opposite of everything I've said today:

"Drink your juice, honey."

"Don't want juice, want milk!"

"Put your socks back on, the floor's cold."

"Don't want socks."

"Get your shoes and we'll go outside."

"Don't want to."

"Okay, let's read a book."

"I wanna go outside."

"Maybe we should take a nap."

"I not sweepy."

"Well Mommy is. . ."

"You sweep; I go get some juice."

I've been firm. I've been patient. I've been as consistent as I know how to be. But when all is said and done, sometimes you just have to get through it.

Toddlers are some of the most unique little beings on earth. One minute you want to cry in frustration and the next you want to eat them up. Isn't it amazing how a bear hug and a few wet kisses can virtually erase a whole day of battles? (Of course I can never tell if the affection is genuine or if she's just softening me up for the next round.)

Father,
I am so tired.
This entire day has been
one long struggle.
Please help me to be consistent
and patient in the coming days.
And help me to remember, Lord,
that these times are only temporary.
With Your guidance they can also
be rich and rewarding.

Therefore, since we are surrounded by such a great cloud of witnesses, let us throw off everything that hinders and the sin that so easily entangles, and let us run with perseverance the race marked out for us.　　　HEBREWS 12:1

TIME OFF

The girls were spending a couple of days with Aunt Charlene and Uncle Dave. Sitting at the kitchen table, I was in complete awe at the stillness and silence in the house. I could actually hear the ticking of our wall clock, a sound which I previously did not know existed. Finishing a leisurely lunch where I savored every uninterrupted bite, I glanced around in satisfaction.

Earlier, I had picked up around the house, and to my complete surprise, things remained clean and clutter-free. No one tracked dirt across the floor, scattered toys in the living room, or painted toothpaste on the bathroom sink.

Almost giddy with the prospect of being alone in my own home, I grabbed a book and snuggled up on the couch to read. Before I knew it, I had absorbed an entire page without having to referee a sibling skirmish or take someone to the potty. *Wow, so this is how the other half lives.*

That evening was equally remarkable. Roy and I actually finished every conversation started. We enjoyed our evening meal without the pressure of making someone eat their veggies while someone else sang at the table. Then we watched the entire evening newscast and read the paper cover to cover. And if that wasn't enough, not having to face the usual bedtime battles left us more energy for each other. We actually stayed up later and cherished some real quality time together.

The next morning dawned on a happier, more well-rested mom. With a song in my heart, I began puttering around the house, enjoying my freedom. About midmorning, however, I realized that the house was a bit too quiet. And I had gone a little too long without any baby arms around my neck. I missed the sound of childish voices filling each room.

Someday, there will come a time when the girls will be grown and gone, and it will be just Roy and me again. I look forward to that time, for I know God has a plan for that part of our lives.

But for now, I'm grateful for where I am, for this time in my life. My years of being "Mama" to little ones are short-lived, and I must cherish each and every God-given day.

Oh Father,
thank You for time alone—
time where I can get reacquainted with
myself, my husband, with You.
Thank You for fresh perspective
on motherhood's calling and
for renewed strength to carry on.

Teach us to number our days aright, that we may gain a heart of wisdom.   PSALM 90:12

ATTITUDE OF GRATITUDE

Give thanks to the LORD, for he is good;
his love endures forever.

PSALM 107:1

I opened the pantry door and stood there staring, hoping a delicious entree would pop out and volunteer to fix itself. With a sigh of boredom, I grudgingly began laying out the ingredients for our evening meal. *I am so tired of fixing dinner every evening,* I thought with a major " 'tude."

As the oven preheated, Katie wrapped herself around my leg and insisted on "helping Mama." Not in the mood for toddler help, I sent her to her room to play. Of course she immediately started to whine and cry because "Mama wouldn't let her help." *Good grief,* I fumed inwardly, *I really don't need this aggravation. I wish I could get off work at five like the rest of the world.*

Suddenly, my thoughts went back in time to the early months of my pregnancy with Katie. After being exposed to poison ivy, I developed a severe rash that eventually covered both legs from the knees down. In addition to the itchy misery, I had a cold and was on several strong medications. Due to my illness and the possible risk to the pregnancy, I was confined to bed for several weeks.

As I thought back to the struggles and frustrations of those difficult weeks, I remembered my one consistent prayer during that time: *Please, Lord, just let me get well so I can take care of my family again.*

Once again, I had slipped into the rut of apathy and discontent. I had been taking for granted the simple joy of serving my family. With a quick prayer of gratitude for His reminder, I asked the Lord for renewed patience. Then with a sigh of resolve, I called to my little one, "Oh Katie-belle, want to help Mama in the kitchen?" (She did.)

Father,
please forgive me for
the times I take for granted
Your gift of motherhood.
Help me to hold in my heart an
"attitude of gratitude"
that I may take joy in
serving You through
my everyday responsibilities.

They were also to stand every morning to thank and praise the LORD. They were to do the same in the evening.

1 CHRONICLES 23:30

In Closing. . .

The one who calls you is
faithful and he will do it.

1 Thessalonians 5:24

I am in no way, shape, or form an expert on motherhood. But my years of serving as a wife and mother have taught me a few invaluable insights:

- For one thing, I've accepted the fact that the closest I've ever come or ever will come to being a Proverbs 31 woman was when I was really sick and my doctor put me on steroids.

- Men are slightly difficult when they're sick.

- Children will say they love you, but they never back it up by keeping their rooms clean.

- Other people (usually strangers) have all the answers when it comes to raising your children.

- The front passenger seat of any vehicle was created for the specific purpose of causing sibling strife.

- My mom's wish that I would have children "just like me" came true.

- The only thing harder than being a mom is. . . um. . .well, actually I haven't discovered it yet.

- And if I could snap my fingers this very moment and become anything in the whole world I wanted to be, I would choose to be exactly what I am: an extremely human, take-one-day-at-a-time, saved-by-grace. . .mom.

Lord,
I want to walk with You.
Not just on Sundays or
special occasions or
when the sun is shining,
but every day, in every way.
And Father, I want to be real.
Not caught up in
tradition or habit or appearances.
I want Your ways,
Your eyes, Your heart.
And in those moments when I have
the privilege of touching another's life,
my deepest desire is to leave
behind the fragrance of You.

Now it is God who makes both us and you stand firm in Christ. He anointed us, set his seal of ownership on us, and put his Spirit in our hearts as a deposit, guaranteeing what is to come.

2 CORINTHIANS 1:21–22

ABOUT THE AUTHOR

Leigh Ann Thomas of North Carolina serves the Lord in many capacities: as a Christian writer and dramatist, and as a wife and mother of three daughters. While she feels a passion for the arts, Leigh Ann believes her "first and highest calling" is serving the Lord in her home. She is the Creative Ministry Team Leader at her church, Cool Springs Baptist, and participates in the Women's Missionary Union.

Time Out is Leigh Ann's second published book. She is also the author of *Go Ye Therefore: Dramas for Today's Church,* published by New Hope Publishers. She has written and performed for the CrossWalk Drama Ministry for seven years and has had a number of dramas published in drama magazines and collections.

Inspirational Library

Beautiful purse/pocket-size editions of Christian classics bound in flexible leatherette. These books make thoughtful gifts for everyone on your list, including yourself!

When I'm on My Knees The highly popular collection of devotional thoughts on prayer, especially for women.
Flexible Leatherette. $4.97

The Bible Promise Book Over 1,000 promises from God's Word arranged by topic. What does God promise about matters like: Anger, Illness, Jealousy, Love, Money, Old Age, and Mercy? Find out in this book!
Flexible Leatherette. $4.97

Daily Wisdom for Women A daily devotional for women seeking biblical wisdom to apply to their lives. Scripture taken from the New American Standard Version of the Bible.
Flexible Leatherette. $4.97

My Daily Prayer Journal Each page is dated and features a Scripture verse and ample room for you to record your thoughts, prayers, and praises. One page for each day of the year.
Flexible Leatherette. $4.97

Available wherever books are sold.
Or order from:

Barbour Publishing, Inc.
P.O. Box 719
Uhrichsville, OH 44683
http://www.barbourbooks.com

If you order by mail, add $2.00 to your order for shipping.
Prices are subject to change without notice.